Toys from
Alice in Wonderland

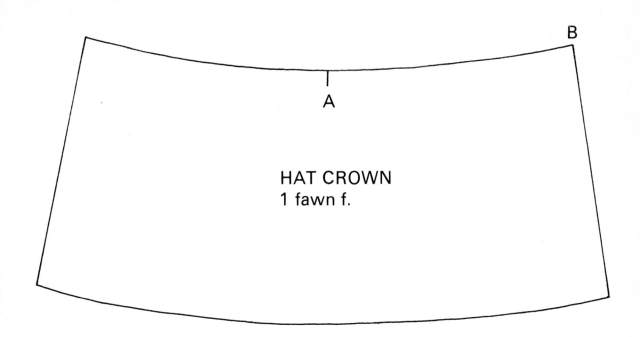

HAT CROWN
1 fawn f.

Toys from Alice in Wonderland

Margaret Hutchings

Mills & Boon Limited,
London, Sydney, Toronto

First published in Great Britain 1979 by
Mills & Boon Limited,
17–19 Foley Street, London W1A 1DR

ISBN 0 263 06400 X (Cased)
0 263 06410 7 (Limp)

Filmset and printed in Great Britain by
BAS Printers Limited, Over Wallop,
Hampshire, and bound by Hunter & Foulis
Limited, Edinburgh.

CONTENTS

ACKNOWLEDGMENTS

Margaret Hutchings, who was taken ill during the course of writing, is particularly grateful for Doris Cook's assistance which enabled her to complete this book.

The author and publisher would also like to thank the late Rudi de Sarigny for her help and advice and are grateful to Ed Dwyer for supplying all the photographs.

All royalties are to be donated to medical research and the book is dedicated with affection and gratitude to all those who have helped the families of Margaret Hutchings and Doris Cook fight a multitude of battles over the years.

GENERAL
INSTRUCTIONS

Before starting work on any of the animals, read first the following general instructions, then the instructions for the toy you have decided to make, checking any cross-references, at the same time turning to and reading through any special processes referred to in the text and making sure you understand what is involved. If you don't own *Alice's Adventures in Wonderland* or *Through the Looking-Glass* borrow them from the library and read the stories before making the characters concerned in them. Always keep the Lewis Carroll books handy for reference while working. In this way you will approach the work with a clear picture in your mind and creating the toy will not only be immensely satisfying but altogether much easier.

CROSS-REFERENCES
In a book of this type where much of the work is repetitive, a large number of cross-references cannot be avoided. The easiest way to deal with this problem is to prepare a number of strips of paper and while reading through the instructions before starting work, slip one into each page referred to, perhaps pencilling a name or number on the end to help you see the correct place at a glance.

METRICATION
Metric measurements are given throughout the book with their approximate

equivalents in inches, yards, ounces etc. in brackets.

PREPARING THE PATTERNS
All the patterns given with the instructions for each toy are full-size and ready to trace (you can nevertheless alter the dimensions if you wish – see following pages 8–9. It

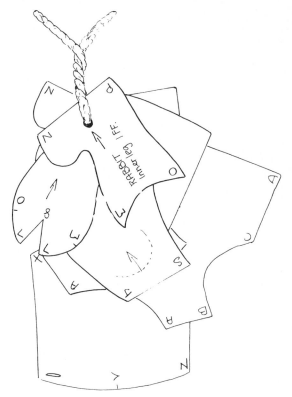

Fig. 1 A set of patterns prepared for storing

is well worth taking time and trouble to prepare these accurately and in a form that can be used many times. When you have decided which toy you are going to make, trace the necessary pattern pieces on to thin cardboard (you can use old cereal boxes for this) and cut out each piece smoothly and carefully. Mark in the arrows, letters, numbers, 'openings', 'folds' and any other directions and label the templets clearly (for example, Mad Hatter, JACKET FRONT, 2 RED). Punch a hole in each piece and thread all the templets together with a pipe-cleaner (Fig. 1). These prepared sets can be stored together in a special box and are always ready for use.

Folds

Watch for the word 'fold' on some of the pieces. This method was found necessary in the case of some of the larger, evenly-shaped patterns in order to save space. It means just what it says – i.e. cut double, folded down the broken line. The best way to do this on thick material like felt or fur fabric is to draw one half, then turn the carboard templet over at the broken 'fold' line and draw the second half. Alternatively, the half pattern can be traced twice on to the cardboard when making the templet so that a complete pattern is made and used normally when cutting out.

Checking the pieces

Some of the animals have quite a lot of small parts, so to help you check that you have cut them all before starting to sew, the final number of pieces is given in each case under 'cut out'. In some cases the pattern pieces for a single toy are taken from more than one character. When this happens several subtotals are given so that you can check the pieces as you go along. The final number is given at the end (e.g. for the White Queen, page 70.

Fig. 2 Enlarging or reducing a pattern

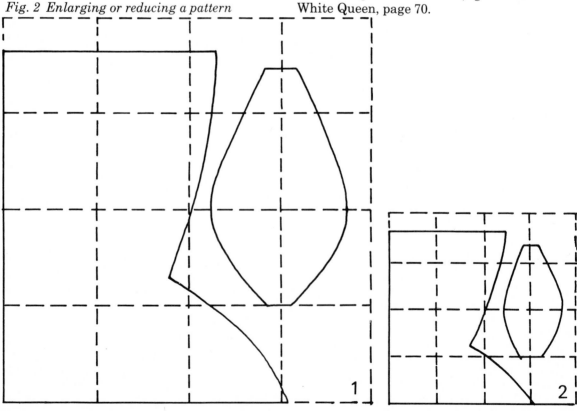

Enlarging or reducing a pattern

There is absolutely no need for any complicated processes if you wish to enlarge or reduce a pattern. All that is necessary is to draw round the pattern concerned on a piece of squared paper, with for instance, 2·5 cm (1 in) squares as in Fig. 2. Then draw exactly the same number of squares each one correspondingly larger (e.g. 5 cm (2 in)) or smaller (e.g. 1·5 cm ($\frac{1}{2}$ in)) as in Fig. 2(1) and (2) and copy each pattern piece on to this paper, making sure that each curve crosses a line in just the same place as it does on the first paper. However, it is important to remember that by making only a small alteration to each of the dimensions of length, width and height you will cause a surprising change in the overall size of the toy.

MATERIALS

You will usually find the felt, fur fabrics and other materials you require in drapers (US dry goods stores), the haberdashery (US notions) department of any large store or in a shop which specializes in needlework equipment. A little imagination is sometimes needed to find certain materials for the toys, but the instructions for each figure list possible sources to help you. The following materials apart from the basic felt or fur fabric will be required for any of the toys you make.

Fillings

Kapok (a natural material which envelops the seeds of a tropical tree) As the toys will not be washable (with the possible exception of the White Rabbit which is not made of felt) there is no doubt that this good old 'standby' takes a great deal of beating. It can be separated into the tiniest wisps and used most successfully for stuffing even such small parts as the beaks of the thimble toys. Always take a small ball of kapok at a time, rolling it in your hand and pushing into place with a stuffing stick of an appropriate size (page 10).

Do not simply fill the body cavities with kapok but stuff firmly and model your toy at the same time taking care to push out nose, cheeks etc., following the diagrams and Tenniel drawings, to give your toy character. If you are at all asthmatical or suffer from catarrh, it is a good idea to tie a mask round your nose before working with this material, as it can have quite a nasty effect. Tiny specks float round the room and have an infuriating habit of rising with the heat and collecting in an almost uncanny fashion in odd corners of the room and round lampshades! The kitchen is therefore the best place to work when you first start using kapok – wearing an apron and a mask – or better still and in good weather, in the garden. After a while you become so used to handling it that you are able to work cleanly, without getting any on you, the outside of the toy or the lampshades!

Man-made fibres For convenience kapok alone is mentioned in the lists of materials for making each toy. However, man-made fibres are very suitable alternatives. Indeed, these modern fillings are so clean that they are a joy to use. Various man-made fillings are available in a range of prices and quality. Whichever you choose be sure to buy the loose, opened form for toy filling, not the sort sold for quilting. Since the fibres in all these materials are unbreakable there is no problem of loose pieces floating in the atmosphere!

NOTE: In the case of the Queen of Hearts and Tweedledum and Tweedledee where a lot of filling is required, an amount is specified to help you when you start to assemble the materials.

Adhesives

The white glue adhesive sold for general purposes will be suitable. Strong clear glue will also be needed to stick wooden parts, as in the case of Alice with a Telescopic Neck.

Wool

The wool is required for hair and unless otherwise stated should be of the thickness of Double Knitting yarn (twice as thick as 4 ply wool).

Thread

For the seams this should be mercerized cotton or polyester thread. Embroidery silks in various colours will be needed for the eyes, noses and other features.

Trimming

A trimming known as Russia Braid is used for many of the toys. In case you have any difficulty in obtaining this and need to find an approximate equivalent Fig. 3 will show you the kind of trimming that is required.

Fig. 3 Russia braid

TOOLS

Pins and needles

Sewing needles, some very fine, and a long darning needle (to enable you to stitch right through the hands of the toys where necessary), pins and a thimble, tailor's chalk and a soft pencil will all be required. A sewing machine, though not essential, will be of great assistance for making long even seams. If you do not have a machine, stitch seams with a firm backstitch.

Stuffing sticks

For stuffing, a blunt length of wood dowelling rod or the handle of a wooden spoon will help you to push the filling well into the bodies of the toys. Orange sticks and pencils will enable you to reach the corners.

Wires

For stiffening legs etc. ordinary galvanized fencing wire will be suitable. However, the ends must be folded back and then bound with strips of adhesive tape (and subsequently with rag if more bulk is required) to prevent any dangerous sharp edges protruding from the toy.

CUTTING OUT

NOTE: The abbreviations f. (felt) and f.f. (fur fabric) are used on pattern pieces where more than one type of material is needed for a toy.

Cutting felt

Place the cardboard templets on the material, trying them this way and that so as to use the felt in the most economical way. Draw round each one with a soft pencil so that no marks are left to show on the finished toy.

Cutting fur fabric

Stroke the material to decide which way the pile turns, then turn it over and pencil a large arrow on the back indicating this direction. Place the card templets on the back of the material, their arrows following the pile of the material and draw all round them with a soft pencil or tailor's chalk. (Ballpoint pen may rub and stain the edges of the pile). Use small, very sharp scissors for cutting, and slide along under the

1 cut fur fabric like this

2 never like this

Fig. 4 Cutting fur fabric

pile in a short, snipping movement to cut only the back of the fabric (Fig. 4(1)) never the pile (2). In this way the pile will be left to mask the seams on the finished toy, much improving its appearance.

Cutting pairs
Some parts are labelled 'cut 1 pair' as opposed to 'cut 2'. This is to remind you that the pattern piece needs to be reversed when cutting one of the parts or both the pieces will be facing in the same direction (e.g. White Rabbit's outer arm on page 20).

STITCHING

Stitching felt
Pin first then sew with a small, fine needle and mercerized cotton or polyester thread which exactly matches the felt. If working on the right side use a small, neat stab stitch or fine oversewing, whichever is recommended in the text for the part in question. On the wrong side either of these stitches may be used, but stab stitch has the advantage of looking neater on the right side when the work is turned. Work very close to the edge of the felt leaving practically no turning (Fig. 5(2) and (3)). Remember to count all pins and any needles used to hold parts while sewing so that none are left in the fabric of the finished toy.

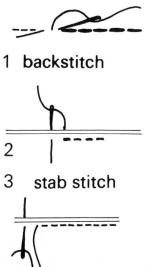

1 **backstitch**

2

3 **stab stitch**

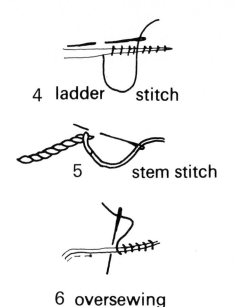

4 **ladder stitch**

5 **stem stitch**

6 **oversewing**

Fig. 5 Various stitches used for toy making and referred to in the text

Stitching fur fabric
Work on the wrong side and always pin first, then tack by carefully oversewing, pushing the pile of the fabric through to the inside as you work (Fig. 6(1–3)). Any colour thread may be used for this tacking for although it is not removed (it adds extra strength to the work), being inside the finished toy it does not show. What better way to use up all those odds and ends on bobbins in the sewing machine and forgotten spools at the bottom of the workbox? After tacking, stitch either by machine or by hand using a firm, strong backstitch. Turnings of just over 0·5 cm ($\frac{1}{4}$ in) have been allowed on all the patterns unless otherwise stated. It is a good idea to have your machine threaded up and handy so that you can tack a pile of pieces while sitting by the fire or in the garden, then machine them as they are ready. However, some small parts such as inserting soles into feet (e.g. Tweedledum and Tweedledee pages 38–39) are obviously easier to cope with by hand.

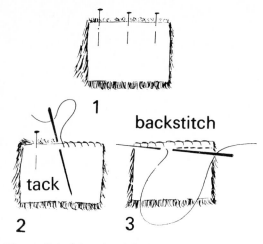

Fig. 6 Stitching fur fabric

Ladder stitch

This extremely useful stitch turns the edges of an opening 'into itself' and is by far the most satisfactory method to use for many toymaking processes. It consists of a small running stitch taken first on one side of an opening then on the other, which when pulled tightly, closes that opening invisibly (Fig. 7). *Never oversew* an opening, as this will make an ugly ridge and the stitches will show. Use ladder stitch also for sewing on arms – a stitch alternately on the arm and body, working all round several times (Fig. 8) – and for joining heads, tails, etc., to a body. Fine thread will eventually break under the strain of the necessary pulling and is therefore useless for this stitch; the limbs will come off and the finished toy will be unsatisfactory. Always use strong button thread in a long needle for ladder stitching

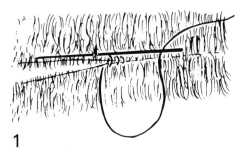

Fig. 7 Closing an opening with ladder stitch

fur fabric and doubled cotton thread or similar in a long, slim needle for ladder stitching felt.

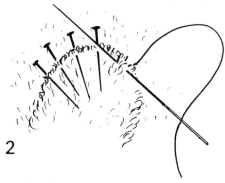

Fig. 8 Ladder stitching a limb to body

Stab stitch

Stab stitch (Fig. 5(2) and (3)) is used on the right side for the toys when the parts are too small to turn after sewing. This stitch is virtually like a very small running stitch, but because felt is too thick a material to 'run' in the accepted sense of the word, the needle is stabbed through backwards and forwards. Use matching polyester or cotton thread for this – a single strand only and a very fine needle. The stitches sink into the felt so as to become almost invisible.

STUFFING

Turning the parts

A blunt orange stick or the wrong end of a pencil is often useful for turning heads, legs, etc. right side out after stitching – sometimes an awkward job. After turning, push out all bulges and corners well before stuffing, but be careful not to pierce the material.

Packing the filling in place

Work slowly and carefully when filling your toy, using only a very small amount of filling at a time and pushing it into place with a stick of a suitable size. Take care to push out any hollows and lumps that may occur as you work, for once you have finished stuffing the only way to correct these is to take out filling and begin again.

Apart from the furry White Rabbit and March Hare whose heads can be reasonably soft, the felt figures must be of rock-like firmness, particularly those which contain any wire. In this case the best plan is to stuff until not one more scrap will go inside and then find room for a little more! However, do not force the filling in too hard as you will only break your stitching or distort the shape of the material.

NEEDLE MODELLING

Needle modelling is absolutely essential to bring out the full character and shape of many of the toys. It is a fascinating process rather like sculpture, whereby dimples, fat cheeks, sunken eyes, etc. are introduced by a series of stitches taken backwards and forwards through the head or part of the body in question and pulled tightly. Strong thread and a long, slim needle are necessary and the picture of the animal you are making as well as the relevant diagram should be carefully followed. Full instructions are given for each toy. However, every worker pulls a little more or less tightly than another and stuffs a little more or less fully, so don't be afraid to consult the pictures in the Lewis Carroll books and continue modelling in your own way until you are absolutely satisfied with your animal's features and characteristics.

FINISHING

Go over all the seams and round the eyes with the blunt end of a large needle or the points of your scissors, pulling out any fur pile that is caught up in the stitching. Now brush the toy thoroughly to remove excess loose threads, stuffing etc. You should always brush felt with a piece of dry foam sponge as this will not disturb the surface of the fabric and is also very good at brushing off kapok.

Finally take a critical look at the collars, sleeve frills, dresses, etc. Are they immaculate and looking as though they have been freshly laundered, or have they become rather limp in the making? A little spray starch and a hot iron will work wonders in restoring a crisp, pristine appearance.

THE WHITE RABBIT

A cuddly toy with three changes of clothes
Height: 35 cm (14 in)

'. . . suddenly a White Rabbit with pink eyes ran close by her.'

Tenniel gives this strange creature human
hands and during the course of *Alice's
Adventures in Wonderland* he appears in
three different costumes. Instructions
follow first for making the basic rabbit then
for each of his sets of clothes and
accessories. You can therefore make all
three sets, which children will love being
able to change whenever they like, or
choose the one which for you is the most
typical. (The White Rabbit's tiny feet make
it impossible for him to stand unsupported.)

MATERIALS
White fur fabric for main parts:
23 cm × 90 cm (9 in × 36 in)
Scraps of pale pink felt for ear linings,
hands and foot pads
Scraps of black and white felt for eyes
Black stranded cotton for claw markings
and nose
Ten pipe-cleaners for stiffening fingers
Four black bristles for whiskers (these can
be pulled out of an old brush)
Kapok for stuffing
Adhesive
Adhesive tape

METHOD
Cut out the pieces as given on pages 19–21
(28 pieces).

Ears Starting on the wrong side of the fur
fabric ear pieces, smear adhesive all round
the outside edge then fold this in as far as
the broken lines and press well down until
dry. Stick a pink felt ear lining on to each
ear. Roll the base of each ear inwards and
stitch in place for about 2·5 cm (1 in)
upwards (see Fig. 1 for shape).

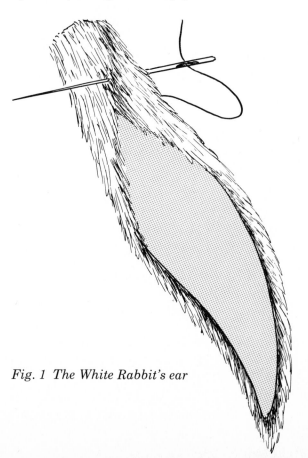

Fig. 1 The White Rabbit's ear

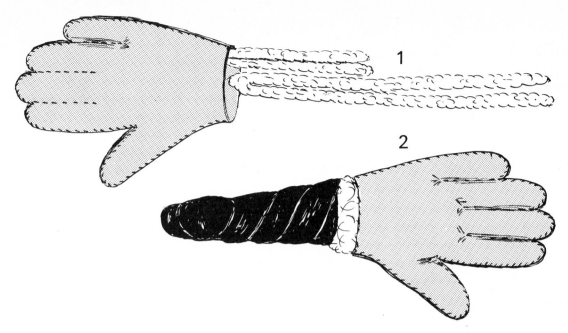

Fig. 2 Making the hands

Hands Place the pieces together in pairs and very neatly join them by oversewing all round outside edge except for short, straight end D–F. Stab stitch the pieces together between the fingers as shown by broken lines on pattern. Fold the ten pipe-cleaners in half and push one into each of the fingers and thumbs with the doubled ends inside (Fig. 2(1)). Now push a little stuffing into each hand on both sides of pipe-cleaners, making one side fatter (this will be the back of the hand) then bind the protruding ends of the cleaners tightly together with adhesive tape, making sure the sharp ends are well covered (Fig. 2(2)).

Arms On each outer arm join the top darts A-B. Place each inner arm on an outer arm, right sides together, and join them C-D and E-F. Turn right side out. Turn back the wrist edge D-F-D to broken line on pattern and tack. Slip a hand into each arm, making sure you have thumbs uppermost matching the D's and F's on hands and arms. Pin in place then stitch firmly all the way round wrists. Stuff arms firmly, making sure that the pipe-cleaners are well embedded, but do not sew up the ends.

Legs Place the inner and outer legs together in pairs and on the wrong side join them G-H-I and J-K. Take the two felt foot pads and insert one into the base of each leg matching I's and K's and stitching all round, taking as small a turning as is safe. Turn the legs right way out. Place them together side by side, feet facing forward and on the wrong side oversew, then backstitch together G-R (as if they were a pair of trousers). Stuff each leg very firmly taking particular care over the feet and ankles.

Tail Place the two pieces together and on the wrong side stitch all round the curved edge. Turn right way out and stuff very lightly. Turn in straight edges marked by broken line on pattern and oversew.

Body and head Take the body gusset and on the wrong side join it to one side of body L-M-N. Join the head gusset to the same side of body L-O just tacking but not stitching the short section marked 'ear' on top of head. Join the other body side to these pieces working round P-O-L-M-N-Q and again tacking but not stitching the ear section. Turn right side out, stuff fully and firmly and close opening.

Assembling Part the pile on the fur fabric over the two places at top of head where the seam is held together by tacking and with small pointed scissors cut the tacking threads, thus making two small openings in the seams. Push a stuffing stick in to make a channel then push an ear firmly into each hole at a backward slant, linings outward, points curling forwards, and ladder stitch firmly in place working all round each ear several times.

Pin the legs in place, experimenting to find the best position for your own particular toy, so that the front seams on legs will match front seams on body. Ladder stitch very firmly in place, working backwards and forwards several times and pushing extra stuffing inside round the tops of legs at the back as you work so as to fill them out well. If you wish you can catch the inner legs together at point H on pattern so that the feet turn outwards. Clip a little fur away from front of feet and embroider four black stitches to indicate divisions between claws (Fig. 3). While you have a needle threaded with black stranded cotton clip a little fur away from tip of nose and embroider nose and mouth (Fig. 4(2)) starting and finishing off as shown for the claws (Fig. 3(1–7)). Pin the arms one each side of body, again experimenting to get the best position then ladder stitch in place, working several times all round each one and pushing in a little more stuffing at the top as necessary. Sew the tail to the lower part of back so that it hangs downwards, then fold it upwards and stitch in this position.

Eyes Stab stitch each black pupil to a pink eye and embroider a white highlight in the position shown on pattern (page 19) after making sure this looks right on your own rabbit. Neatly hem the completed eyes to each side of head, pushing a little stuffing under each to make it bulge slightly. Then with a long slim needle and strong white thread take a few stitches right through the head from just in front of one eye to the same position on the other side, pulling the stitches tightly to sink the eyes slightly at the front (Fig. 4(1)). Using the blunt end of your needle work all round the outline of each eye, pulling out any pile caught up in the stitching so as to soften the outline. (Look at Fig. 4 and at the eye shown on pattern piece and note the improvement after sinking the eye and softening the outline!)

Finishing off You may like to give your rabbit puffy cheeks, particularly if you intend dressing him as the herald at Alice's trial, in which case he will be blowing a trumpet. If so, cut out two circles of white fur fabric (pattern page 29) gather all round the edge, push a little stuffing inside and pull up gathers slightly to form a little ball. Sew one to each side of mouth, ladder stitching all round several times (Fig. 4(2)).

Fig. 3 Embroidering the paw markings

1 Use a long slim needle: thread up the material to be used and push needle into limb at any position you wish
2 Pull needle and thread through carefully until only a tiny 'end' shows
3 Continue pulling until the end of the thread just disappears inside the limb
4 Push needle back into limb into the same hole from which you have just pulled it out but bring it into a new position
5 Pull needle out, leaving no stitch showing
6 Repeat (4), bringing needle out in yet another position. Continue in this way until no amount of tugging will pull the thread out
7 Push the needle into limb by the same hole from which it has just emerged and bring it out at the place where you wish to embroider
8 Work the paw markings
9 Bring the needle out at any position on the limb
10 Repeat (4) as many times as is necessary to make thread absolutely secure
11 Cut thread close to limb
12 Leaving no end or mark showing

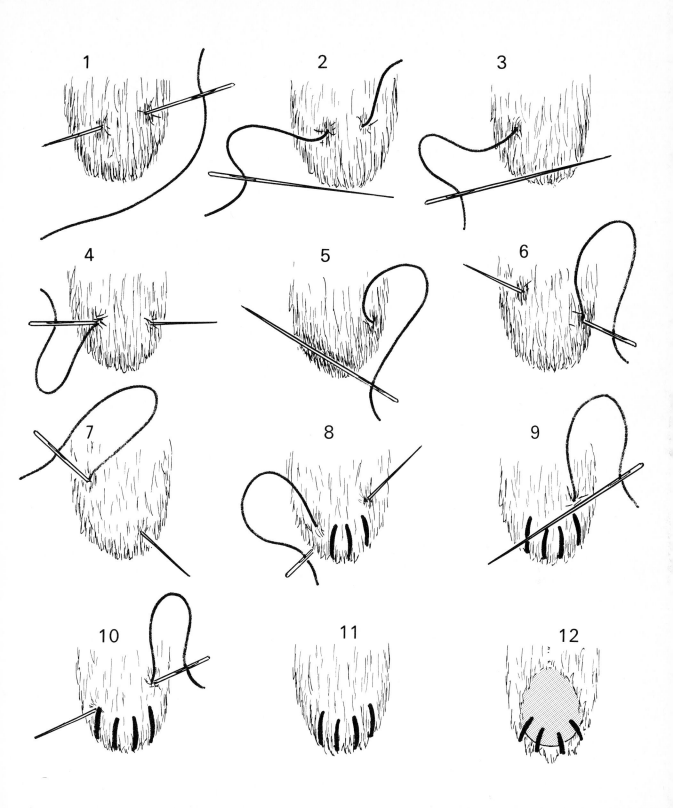

If you wish to add whiskers put a dab of colourless adhesive or nail varnish on the fold of each of the four hairpin-shaped bristles (Fig. 4(3)). For extra strength then stitch two to each side of nose (4), pulling the stitches tightly and working right through nose from one side to the other so as to make it narrower and give it a better shape. Trim whiskers to required length.

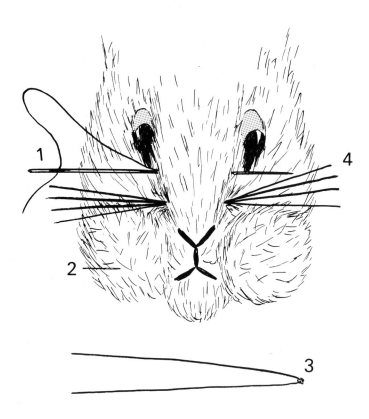

Fig. 4 Sewing the features

THE WHITE RABBIT

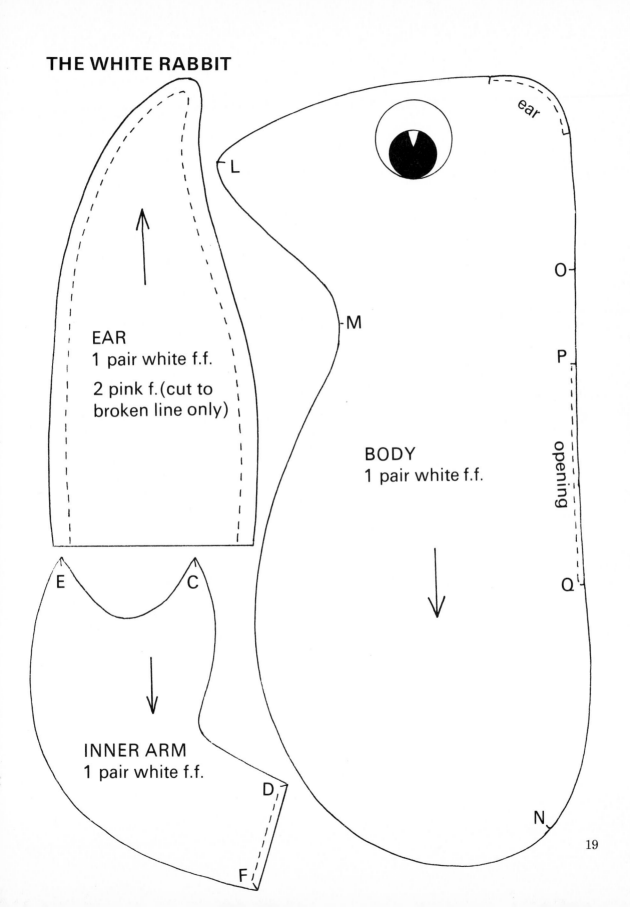

ear

L

O

P

opening

Q

M

EAR
1 pair white f.f.

2 pink f. (cut to
broken line only)

BODY
1 pair white f.f.

E

C

D

F

N

INNER ARM
1 pair white f.f.

19

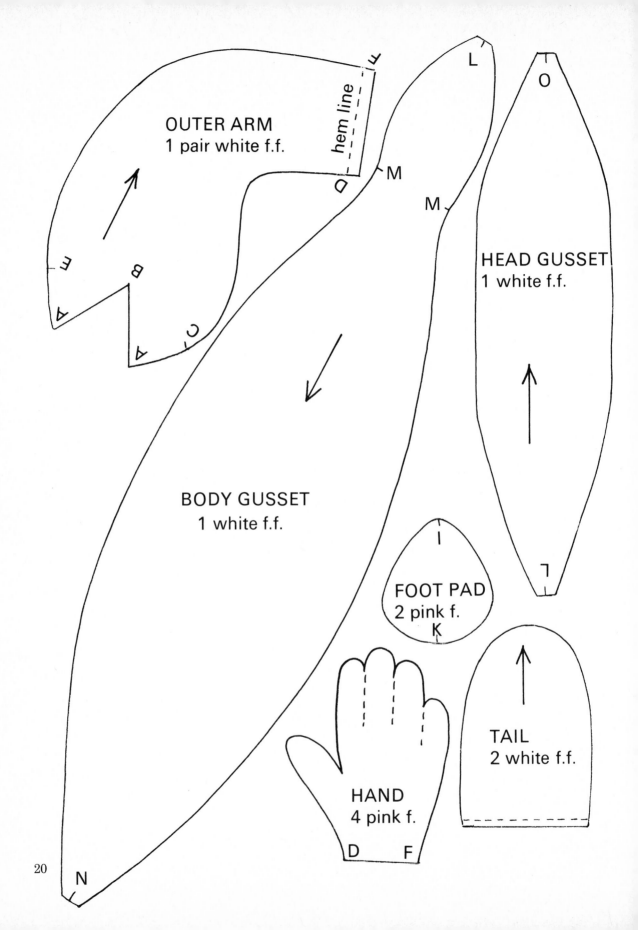

OUTER ARM
1 pair white f.f.

hem line

BODY GUSSET
1 white f.f.

HEAD GUSSET
1 white f.f.

FOOT PAD
2 pink f.

HAND
4 pink f.

TAIL
2 white f.f.

20

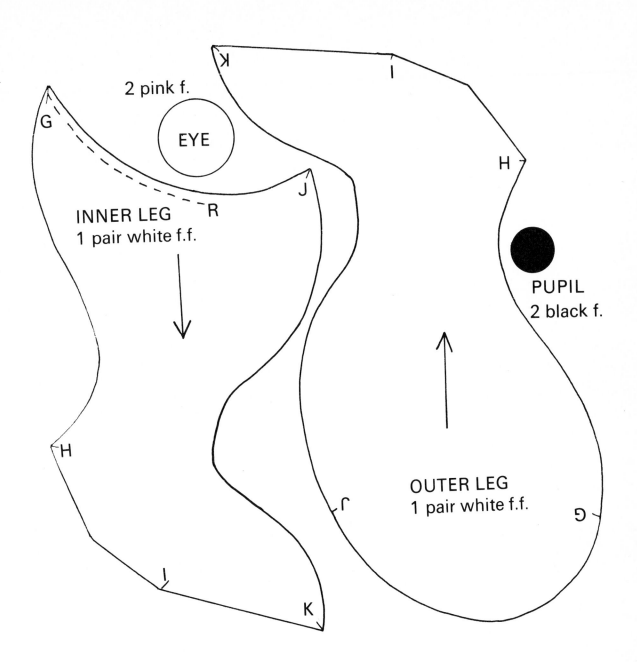

2 pink f.

EYE

INNER LEG
1 pair white f.f.

PUPIL
2 black f.

OUTER LEG
1 pair white f.f.

21

THE WHITE RABBIT AS A COUNTRY SQUIRE

'. . . the Rabbit actually took a watch out of its waistcoat-pocket, and looked at it. . . .'

MATERIALS

Small-checked material for coat:
23 cm × 90 cm (9 in × 36 in)
(this must be lightweight but look 'woolly'
– a wool/cotton mixture is ideal – you could
use part of an old coat lining or warm shirt)
Three small matching buttons for coat
Mustard coloured felt for waistcoat:
23 cm × 23 cm (9 in × 9 in)
Three very small pearl buttons for
waistcoat
A scrap of white felt ⎫
One small snap-fastener or button ⎬ for collar
Grey or beige ribbon for the cravat:
5 cm × 38 cm (2 in × 15 in)
(or a small strip of material with a very
narrow hem all round the edge)
An odd length of fine chain or gold cord
A heavy shank button about 2·5 cm (1 in)
diameter for watch
Adhesive

METHOD

Cut out the pieces as given on page 24 (11 pieces). Now cut out also four coat sleeves and two coat backs as given for the Rabbit Dressed for the Duchess on pages 33–34 (6 pieces). There will be 17 pieces in all. NOTE: Because you are using a material which frays instead of felt the five pieces for

the coat, but not including the collar, should be cut about 0·5 cm (¼ in) larger to allow extra for turnings.

Collar Make a buttonhole on one collar flap and sew a button on to the other, first trying it on to your toy so as to make sure it fits tightly round his neck. Put on the collar and fold the piece of ribbon for the cravat in place.

Waistcoat Make as given for the Rabbit Dressed for the Duchess on page 30 using only three buttons. Sew a small patch pocket to the left side as shown on pattern, making this just large enough to hold the button you have chosen as the basis for his watch. Put the waistcoat on to the Rabbit tucking the cravat in at the top.

Watch Sew one end of the chain to the shank at back of button. Cut a circle of stiff, white paper the same size as the button and stick to the smooth side. Mark the hours all round the edge, with a real watch as a guide, using black ink and a fine pen. Stick a scrap of the mustard felt left over from the waistcoat to cover the back of the button, having the chain coming up between the button and felt and emerging at the top at twelve o'clock. The felt should just show all round the watch face at front. Sew the other end of chain to the middle button on waistcoat and put the watch in the pocket. It can be taken out later and held in the Rabbit's right hand.

Coat The coat is made double then turned, so before starting pencil the actual outline of the pattern shape on to the material pieces (except the collar) and do all the stitching on this line, leaving the extra material you allowed when cutting for turnings. Make up two separate coats in this way (one for the outside and one for the lining). On the wrong side join darts on back X-Y. Join fronts to backs on shoulder seams G-H. Insert sleeves into armholes E-G-E. Sew underarm and side seams F-E-I.

Now place the two coats together pushing one sleeve inside the other) right sides facing and still on the wrong side join them J-P-Q-I-R-S-R-I-Q-P-J all round the

outside edge but leaving the neck edge open. Measure sleeve length to make it fit your toy, turn the outside sleeve back and press, then turn in and slip stitch the lining over it all round lower edge. Turn coat right side out through neck opening, pushing out all the points well with an orange stick and press edges and seams. Stitch the two collar pieces together all round long broken line on pattern. Turn right side out, push out points and press. Pin, tack, then stitch one thickness of collar to the *outside* of coat, matching J-K-J and easing to fit. Then turn in the second (inside) piece and slip stitch to inside of coat J-K-J. Press back revers. Sew three buttons in place, make corresponding buttonholes and put on to Rabbit, leaving the coat undone so that he can handle and consult his watch.

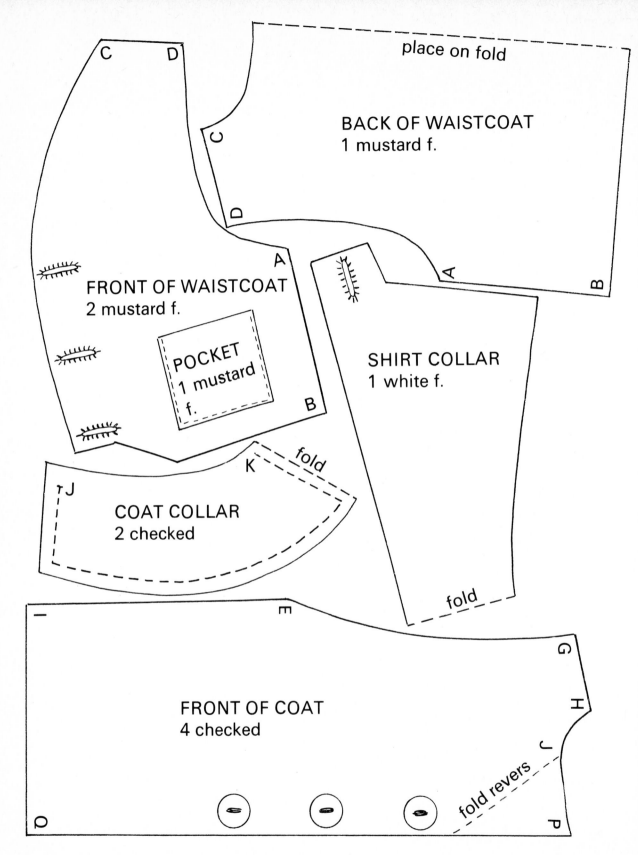

place on fold

BACK OF WAISTCOAT
1 mustard f.

C D

C

D

A

FRONT OF WAISTCOAT
2 mustard f.

A

B

POCKET
1 mustard
f.

B

SHIRT COLLAR
1 white f.

fold

K

J

COAT COLLAR
2 checked

fold

I

E

G

H

J

FRONT OF COAT
4 checked

fold revers

O

P

24

THE WHITE RABBIT AS A HERALD

'. . . near the King was the White Rabbit, with a trumpet in one hand, and a scroll of parchment in the other.'

MATERIALS

Blue felt for tabard and banner:
30 cm × 15 cm (12 in × 6 in)
Scraps of red and yellow felt for trimmings and trumpet
Yellow Russia braid for trimming:
1·8 metres (2 yards)
Iron-on interfacing for stiffening tabard:
25 cm × 15 cm (10 in × 6 in)
Red felt for shirt and tabard lining:
37 cm × 30 cm (15 in × 12 in)
White tape: 2·5 cm × 70 cm
(1 in × 27 in) or a small piece of very } for ruff
thick white interfacing material
Short piece of shirring elastic
White tape for sleeve frills:
1·5 cm × 51 cm ($\frac{1}{2}$ in × 20 in)
About 9 cm ($3\frac{1}{2}$ in) of thin knitting ⎫
needle complete with knob   ⎬ for
Short piece of narrow yellow   ⎭ trumpet
lampshade fringe
Paper clip width of banner
Piece of stiff white paper: ⎫
10 cm × 19 cm (4 in × 7$\frac{1}{2}$ in) ⎬ for
Small red button   ⎭ scroll
Short piece of red wool or fine cord
Red sealing wax
One snap-fastener for shirt
Adhesive

Optional A few cream-coloured ⎫
buttons   ⎬ for plate
Scraps of red felt   ⎭ of tarts
One large coat button

METHOD

Cut out the pieces as given on page 29
(8 pieces without the puffy cheeks) and the
shirt on page 34 using red felt (1 piece)
making 9 pieces in all.

Shirt This goes under the tabard so that
only the sleeves show. Slit up centre line X-
Y on front of shirt only. Join side seams
A-B. Fold each sleeve in half and stitch
underarm seam A-C. Turn sleeve right way
out and slip each one into armholes, pin in
place matching letters then stitch all round
D-A-D. Overlap the two fronts of the shirt
at X and fasten with a small snap-fastener.
Cut the tape for sleeve frills in half and join
the ends of each piece, forming two rings.
Gather all along one edge, pull up to fit
wrist edge of shirt sleeve and fasten off
gathers. Pin the edge of each frill to the
right side of each sleeve arranging the
gathers evenly all round, having the frill
turned back over the bottom of the sleeve
and away from the hand. Oversew in place

all round each sleeve. (Fig. 5) Put the shirt on the Rabbit.

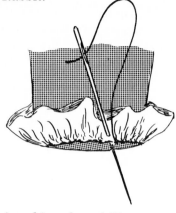

Fig. 5 Attaching sleeve frills

Tabard Stitch the yellow Russia braid in place on the main part and on the epaulets, making front and back of main part alike. It is easiest to attach the two centre crosspieces first, folding the raw ends to the back, then stitch braid all round the edge, not bothering to hem the ends as they will eventually be covered by the epaulets. Make the join on the epaulets' braid at B, leaving the ends raw where they will be covered by bows. Cut out four large and twenty-six small hearts in red felt. Keep each of these in position on the tabard by placing with a tiny spot of adhesive in the centre then hemming neatly all round the edge. Back the main part with iron-on interfacing. Stitch the epaulets in place overlapping main part and matching B's on shoulder and A's on front and back. Find the centre of each shoulder ribbon and sew one to each top of epaulet at B. Tie in a bow, arrange neatly and stitch firmly here and there if necessary. Line the tabard by

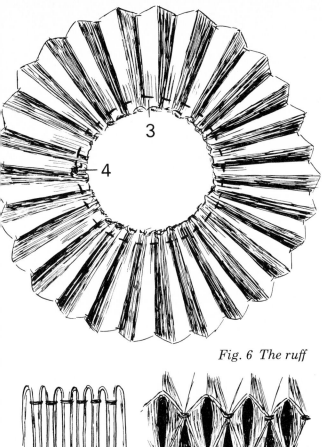

Fig. 6 The ruff

type material you have by you. Joins, if neatly made, will not show on the finished work and will probably be necessary to get the required length. If your material has raw, fraying edges make the smallest, neatest hem possible along both sides so that the completed strip is the required length and width and press well before starting to sew.

Fold the material in a series of pleats 2·5 cm (1 in) deep, catching the pleats together as shown, just a little below the top of each one alternately at top and bottom (Fig. 6(1)), so that when you stretch the work it pulls in and out and when extended looks like (2). Continue in this way all along one edge. Join the ends together as invisibly as possible, cutting a little material off if necessary so as to keep the general pattern of pleating. A honeycomb pattern will show all round the outside of frill. Now on the other edge (i.e. nearest the neck) run shirring elastic through the top of each pleat – one piece through one side (3) and one piece through the other, thus catching the pleats together. Try the ruff on to Rabbit and tie off each piece of elastic very securely (4) so that it fits round his neck and may easily be put on and off. Cut off ends of elastic and put the ruff on to Rabbit. NOTE: The ruff looks the same top and bottom. Fig. 6 shows it as if lying flat; if turned over it would look exactly the same.

Scroll Roll the paper up lengthwise and stick the edge in place just at the centre where the Rabbit's hand will hold it, leaving the corners loose. Bind a piece of thick red wool, fine cord or Russia braid round centre of scroll leaving about 3 cm (just over 1 in) hanging down. Fasten this end to a red button with red sealing wax, then completely cover both sides of button with the wax, pressing it well into place to look like a seal (Fig. 7). Curl the Rabbit's left hand round so that he can hold the scroll firmly.

smearing adhesive all over the main part, laying it on to a piece of red felt and pressing firmly in place. When dry cut away surplus and cut out neck hole. It is best to leave the epaulets unlined or they become too stiff. Put the tabard on to Rabbit.

Ruff For the original a strip of the very thickest interfacing obtainable was used. You may prefer to use tape or strong, crisp ribbon or to make a strip from some cotton

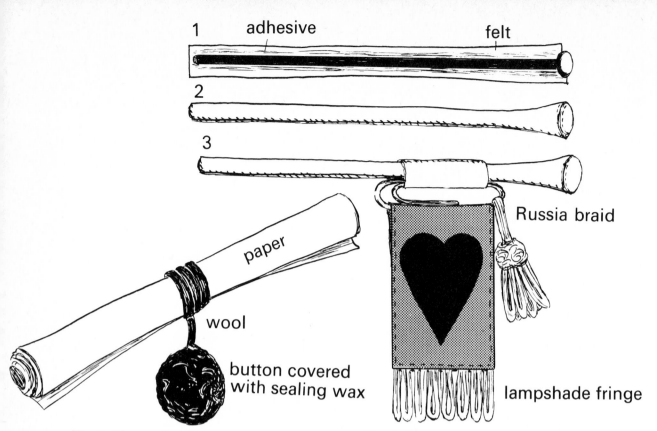

1 adhesive   felt

2

3   Russia braid

paper

wool

button covered
with sealing wax   lampshade fringe

Fig. 7 The scroll   *Fig. 8 The trumpet*

Trumpet Smear a little adhesive on the top of the knob of the knitting needle and stick on a small circle of yellow felt to cover it. Then smear a little adhesive all along one side of knitting needle and lay it on a narrow strip of yellow felt (Fig 8(1)). Roll the felt tightly round and oversew over broken end and along the length. Stab stitch all round top end, attaching strip to circle on end of knob thus making trumpet shape (2). (The adhesive will have prevented the felt slipping on the shiny knitting needle as you work.)

Cut out the two red hearts. Fold the banner in half as shown on pattern and stitch a heart to each side, slip the banner through a paper clip (Fig. 8(3)) and stitch its two sides together all round the three edges, slipping a piece of narrow yellow lampshade fringe between the two bottom edges so that the solid part is hidden and the fringe hangs down. Attach the banner to the trumpet by slipping a small piece of yellow felt through the top of the paper

clip, taking it round the trumpet and oversewing along top. Make a tassel by rolling 3 cm (1 in) of fringe round the end of a short piece of Russia braid like that used on the tabard and stitching it in place. Slip the other end of braid through the front of paper clip holding the banner, fold it down and stitch to itself. Put the trumpet into Rabbit's hand with the end to his mouth.

'. . . the White Rabbit blew three blasts on the trumpet, and then unrolled the parchment scroll, and read as follows:

"The Queen of Hearts, she made some tarts,
    All on a summer day:
    The Knave of Hearts, he stole those tarts,
    And took them quite away!"'

If you would like to make some tarts to go with your toy, find some cream-coloured trouser buttons for pastry and stick circles of red felt to the centre for jam. Pile them on to a large coat button for a plate and stick in place with strong glue.

THE WHITE RABBIT AS A HERALD

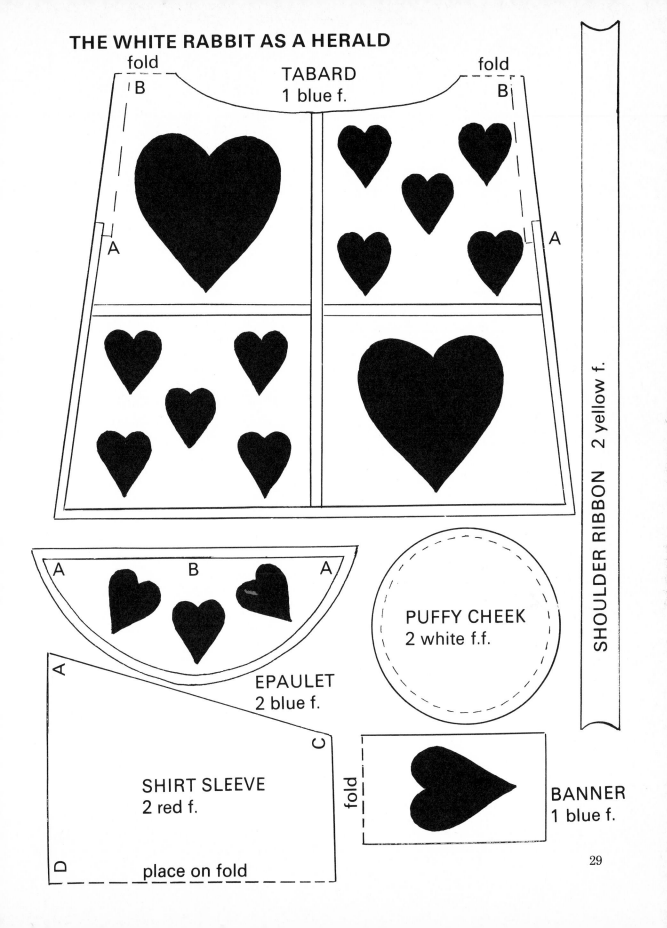

fold

B

fold

B

TABARD
1 blue f.

A

A

SHOULDER RIBBON 2 yellow f.

A   B   A

EPAULET
2 blue f.

PUFFY CHEEK
2 white f.f.

A

C

SHIRT SLEEVE
2 red f.

fold

BANNER
1 blue f.

D   place on fold

29

THE WHITE RABBIT DRESSED FOR THE DUCHESS

'. . . It was the White Rabbit . . . splendidly dressed, with a pair of white kid gloves in one hand and a large fan in the other. . . .'

MATERIALS

Jade green felt (or any bright colour) for the waistcoat: 23 cm × 23 cm (9 in × 9 in)
White felt for the shirt and gloves:
23 cm × 31 cm (9 in × 12 in)
(fine white material may be used instead but in this case allow turnings when cutting out)
Magenta felt (or any bright colour) for coat:
38 cm × 31 cm (15 in × 12 in)
Ten very small buttons
One small snap-fastener
White lace for jabot:
7 cm × 46 cm (2½ in × 18 in)
White lace for cuffs:
2·5 cm × 51 cm (1 in × 20 in)
Russia braid for trimming (white or any colour): 0·4 metres (1½ yards)
Scrap of pretty gauze or lace material (small patterned paper may be used if this not available)
Stiff white plastic (this can be cut from yoghurt pots, ice cream or margarine cartons)
Clear adhesive

} for fan

METHOD

Cut out the shirt sleeves as given for Herald page 29, only in white felt, shirt front and back page 34 (3 pieces), fronts of waistcoat page 34, back of waistcoat and coat collar on page 32 (4 pieces), the sleeves, fronts and back of coat as given on pages 33 and 34 (5 pieces) and the hand pieces as given on page 20 but using white felt as these will be used for the gloves (4 pieces). You should have 16 pieces in all. Do not cut out the fan yet.

Shirt Make the shirt as given for The Rabbit as a Herald on page 25 but using white felt. Make the frills at sleeve edges of fine white lace instead of tape and after oversewing them in place (Fig. 5) turn them downwards so that they will partially cover the Rabbit's hands. To make the jabot, find the centre of the wide piece of lace and pin one edge to centre of back of shirt. Oversew the lace in place all round shirt neck leaving the long ends hanging at front. Put the shirt on the Rabbit, arrange the lace in soft folds round his neck and tie in a large floppy bow under his chin.

Waistcoat Join the fronts to the back on the wrong side, stitching side and shoulder seams A-B and C-D. Turn right side out. Sew four small buttons to one side of front and make corresponding buttonholes on the other. Put waistcoat on to Rabbit, pulling the lace jabot out to hang over it.

Coat Stitch the braid on to sleeves as shown on pattern, leaving ends raw. On the wrong side join underarm seams E-F. Turn sleeves right side out and place on one side. On the wrong side close the two darts on back of coat X-Y. Join the two fronts to the back, stitching shoulder seams H-G and side seams E-I. On the wrong side oversew the collar in place, easing to fit, J-K-J. Starting on one front at point L which will eventually be hidden under the revers, stitch braid down front edge of coat, along lower back edge up and down round back slit and along to the corresponding revers on the second side. Press back revers as shown by broken line on pattern, also the collar at back. At the same time press the side and shoulder seams. Stitch braid round the edge of revers and collar, starting and

finishing on the wrong side just inside fronts of coat where it will not show. Stitch in sleeves matching G-E-G. Sew two buttons to each side of coat and two to the back above slit. Put on to Rabbit so that his tail shows through the back slit and the open front reveals his waistcoat. Pull the lace frills of the shirt sleeves down through coat sleeves so that they fall over the hands.

Gloves The Rabbit cannot wear these of course, but they look very effective when he carries them. On one pair of the pieces (the backs) embroider three short black lines as tucks (Fig. 9). On the other pair (the fronts) sew a tiny button if available, cut a small slit for a buttonhole and work buttonhole stitch round it. Cut a slit down centre of glove. Place each back on top with a front and stab stitch together on the right side, working all round except for the short straight end. Also stitch between fingers as indicated on pattern. Place the gloves in the Rabbit's left hand, curling his fingers round so that he holds them securely.

Fan Cut out the fan shape (pattern page 33) from gauze material. Cut the nine stays from the stiff white plastic. Smear clear adhesive all over the fan then lay the stays in place as shown on Fig. 10 with a little dab of adhesive between each one where they overlap at the handle end. The adhesive on the material will stop the edges fraying as well as holding the stays in place. When quite dry put the fan into the Rabbit's right hand.

'The Duchess! The Duchess! Oh my dear paws! Oh my fur and whiskers! She'll get me executed, as sure as ferrets are ferrets! Where *can* I have dropped [my gloves and fan], I wonder?'

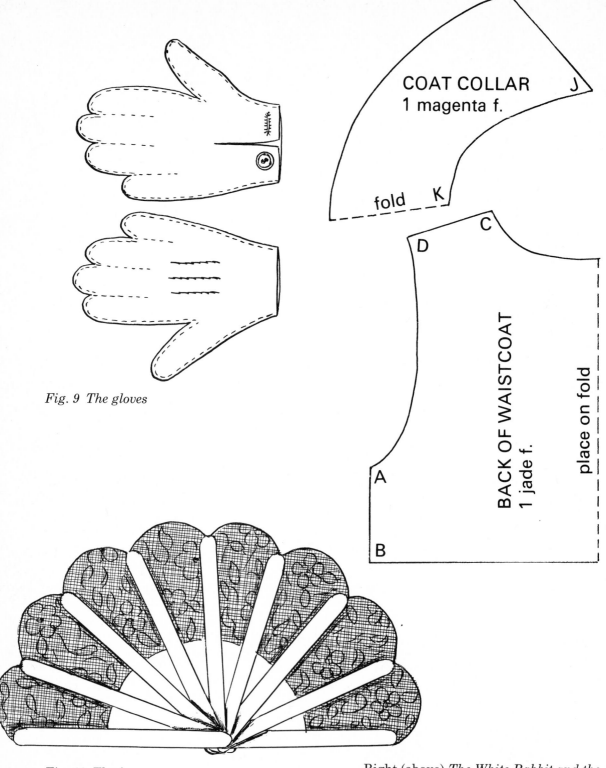

Fig. 9 The gloves

COAT COLLAR
1 magenta f.

J

fold K

C

D

BACK OF WAISTCOAT
1 jade f.

place on fold

A

B

Fig. 10 The fan

Right (above) *The White Rabbit and the
White Rabbit as a Country Squire*
(below) *The Rocking-Horse-Fly*

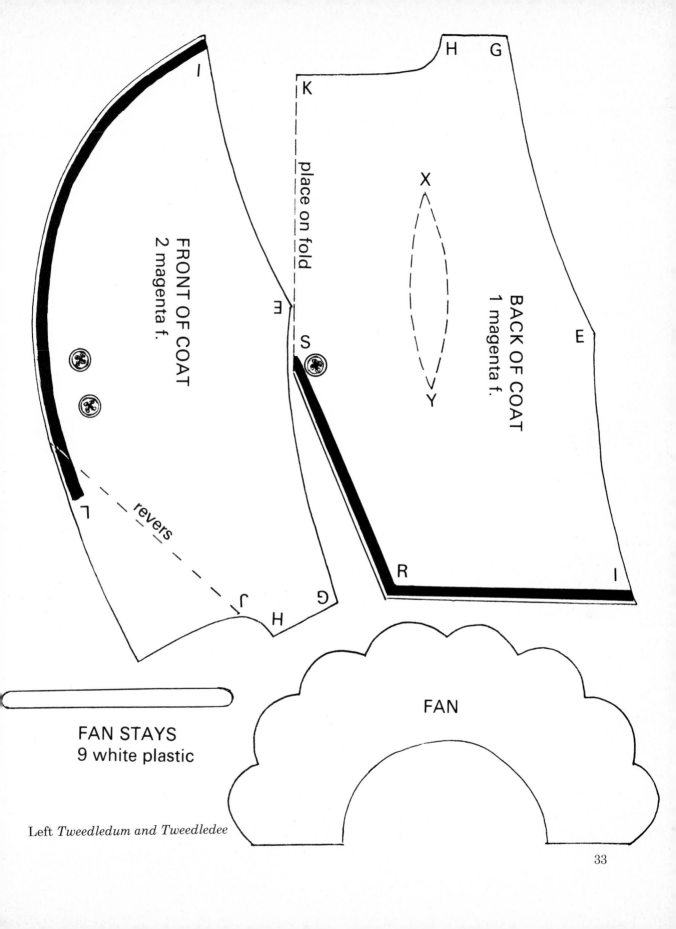

FRONT OF COAT
2 magenta f.

I

place on fold

revers

L

J

G

H

K

E

BACK OF COAT
1 magenta f.

X

Y

S

R

I

FAN

FAN STAYS
9 white plastic

Left *Tweedledum and Tweedledee*

33

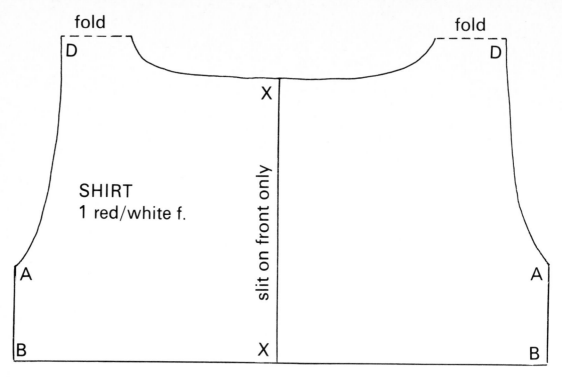

fold   fold

D   D

X

SHIRT
1 red/white f.

slit on front only

A   A

B   X   B

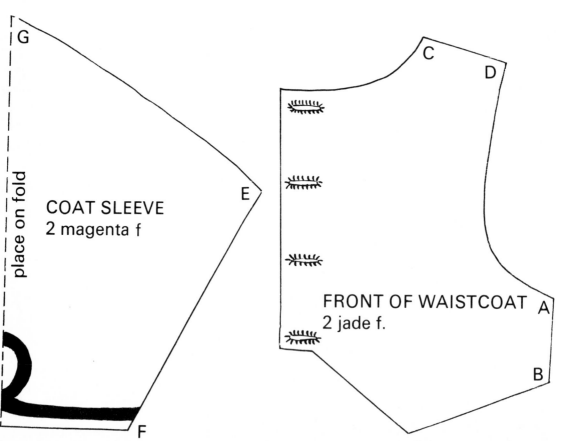

G

COAT SLEEVE
2 magenta f

place on fold

E

C

D

FRONT OF WAISTCOAT
2 jade f.

A

B

F

34

TWEEDLEDUM AND TWEEDLEDEE

Two standing felt toys
Height: 31 cm (12 in)

'They were standing under a tree, each with an arm round the other's neck, and Alice knew which was which in a moment, because one of them had "DUM" embroidered on his collar and the other "DEE". "I supposed they've each got 'TWEEDLE' round at the back of the collar," she said to herself.'

These two fat little men are fastened to each other and to their board with snap-fasteners so that they may be taken apart and put together at will. Their heads and bodies are basically felt balls.

MATERIALS (sufficient for both twins)
Flesh-pink felt for heads and hands:
30 cm × 30 cm (12 in × 12 in)
Royal blue felt for jackets and caps:
35 cm × 35 cm (14 in × 14 in)
Grey felt for trousers:
30 cm × 46 cm (12 in × 18 in)
Scraps of black, white and yellow felt for shoes, caps and eyes
Four pieces of white felt (or any thick material) for socks:
each 7 cm × 24 cm (3 in × 9½ in)
Scraps of white felt and iron-on interfacing material
Scraps of red ribbon for bow ties
Scraps of white cotton trimming for shirt cuffs
Scraps of black or brown fur or fur fabric for hair
Eighteen very small white pearl buttons
Twenty pipe-cleaners for stiffening fingers

Wire for stiffening legs: 36 cm (14 in) long
Eight medium and ten large snap-fasteners
Card of cereal box thickness to back snap-fasteners
Strong cardboard such as the backing of a pad of notepaper } for base
Piece of green material
Black and red embroidery thread for eyebrows, mouths, shoe laces and names on collars
Kapok for stuffing: about 225 kg (8 oz)
Adhesive
Adhesive tape

METHOD

Cut out the pieces as given on page 42 (42 pieces). These will make *one* twin. Double the quantities to make both.

Head On the wrong side join the four sections along the curved edges A-B, leaving a small section of *one* seam open where shown on pattern. Turn right way out. Stuff very firmly and close opening. You now have a ball.* Gather all round the edge of the nose circle, and put a little knob of kapok in the centre. Pull up gathers and fasten off to form a tiny ball. Sew this securely to the head where points A meet.

In order to make sure the twins' faces are exactly alike it is a good idea to make the second head now, then model the features on both at the same time. With a long needle and matching doubled thread take a series of stitches up and down, pulling them tightly to make a little protruding chin (Fig. 1(1)). This should be triangular shape and 3 cm (just over 1 in) below nose. Then take several stitches from each eye position through to top back of head, pulling them

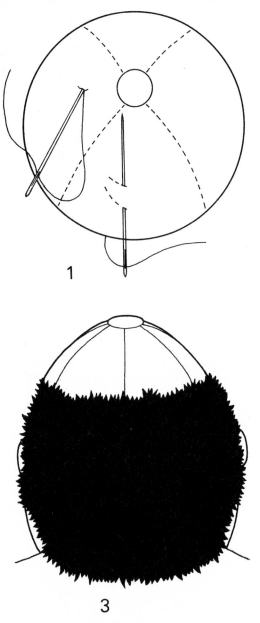

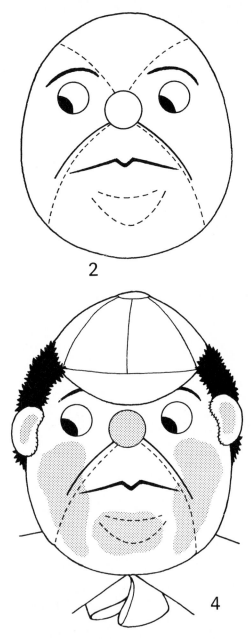

Fig. 1 Tweedledum and Tweedledee – the head

36

tightly to make depressions. You will of course make strange dents on the back of head but these do not matter as they will not show. Stick black pupils to the whites of the eyes, then stick the completed eyes to the head, pressing them well on and into the depressions and stitching to secure (2). Embroider black brows, red mouth and two long lines to represent folds, using thread which exactly matches the colour of the face, following Fig. 1(2) for positions. As you work, pummel and model the head so that it becomes narrower at the top and wider at the bottom.

Cut a piece of black fur fabric to completely cover back of head and stick it in place for hair, tucking the raw edges under as you work and pressing well in place. The hair must come well down at the back so that it will eventually meet collar and high up on top so that the cap will cover the edge at the back (3). No hair shows under the cap at the front.

Cap On the wrong side join the blue and yellow sections alternately C-D. Turn right way out. Stick a tiny circle of yellow felt to the top over joins at C. On the right side oversew the two peak pieces together along curved edge shown by broken line on pattern then slip the edge of cap between these two thicknesses, having the join between two of the sections at centre point of straight edge of peak, pin then neatly stitch peak to cap first on the right side, then on the wrong side. Fill the cap very full of kapok and pin to head, noting that the peak comes well down, almost touching the nose. Stitch the sides and back of the cap, but not the peak, then push in as much extra kapok as you possibly can, smear the underside of the peak with adhesive and stick to forehead. With the points of your scissors tease the pile of the fur out from under the back of the cap so that the edge is buried in hair (3). Stick the ears together in pairs, thus giving them extra bulk, then

stitch an ear to each side of head (4).

To make the twins as lifelike as possible a certain amount of tinting on the face will be needed. Cochineal was used for the originals but water coloured with red paint may be used. Thoroughly wet the parts to be tinted before beginning, as this helps the colour to run and merge on the felt in the most natural way possible. Apply very weak, watered down, colour sparingly with a small paint brush, brushing it well in and following Fig. 1(4) as a guide. Leave it to dry and if necessary repeat. Do remember two important points when using this process. First, you must start by using the colour very sparingly indeed – you can always add more but it is impossible to remove any gaudy red marks you may make by mistake. If this happens your toy will be ruined. Second, take great care not to put the tint near the eyes – if it should run on to the whites of the eyes, again your toy will be ruined and will take on a tipsy, bloodshot look.

Place on one side to dry, preferably overnight, while you make the other parts.

Body Make as for head as far as *, having the two grey sections at the base for trouser tops and the two blue sections at the top for jacket. Place the opening at the top

between the two blue sections where it will eventually be hidden by joining head to body.

Hands and Arms Make the hands as given for the White Rabbit on page 15, but slip a whole pipe-cleaner with one end pinched back (not doubled), into each finger (see Fig. 2(1)). Twist all the protruding cleaners together and sew edge of hand to the cleaners (2). Sew a small piece of white cotton trimming, gathered round each wrist to make a frilly shirt cuff (3). The extreme edge of a piece of broderie anglaise would be very suitable.

On the wrong side join sleeve seams E-F. Turn right way out. Slip sleeves over pipe-cleaners protruding from hands and stitch edges all round wrists so that they cover the gathered raw edge of the shirt cuffs. Stuff fairly firmly so that the cleaners are well embedded in the centre, but do not make the arms so full that they are not reasonably flexible. Sew one half of a medium-sized snap-fastener to each hand (the same halves) as in Fig. 2(3). Put the other two halves aside for later use.

Legs and Feet Place each cardboard sole (the card should be strong) in the centre of a piece of black felt cut a little larger (Fig. 3(1)). Gather round edge and pull up

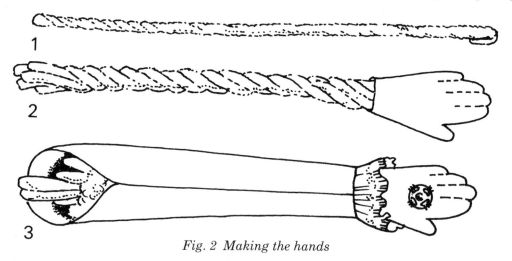

Fig. 2 Making the hands

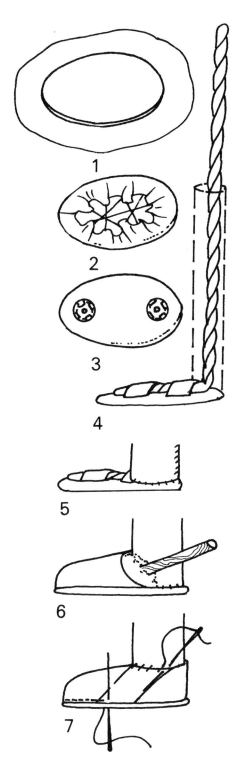

1

2

3

4

5

6

7

Fig. 3 Making the legs

tightly. Fasten off with a few criss-crossed stitches on the wrong side (2). Separate four large snap-fasteners and sew the same half of each to each end of the right side of soles, using plenty of strong, black thread and working right through the felt and the cardboard soles (3). These will fasten each twin to the base later. Keep the opposite halves of the snap-fasteners carefully for use later.

Cut two pieces of wire each 18 cm (7 in) long and bind them with adhesive tape (see Fig. 3(4)). These are to stiffen the legs. Bend approximately 3.5 cm (1½ in) forward at one end for the foot and fasten this securely to the inside of sole with small pieces of adhesive tape. The narrow end of sole (X on pattern) is the toe. Wind a strip of white felt or other white material tightly round the lower part of each leg wire, seaming it up the back (5). Ladder stitch the base of the roll to the black felt on inside of sole. These are for the socks, and the object is to have the rolls just fat enough to make the trouser legs fit tightly at their narrowest part (Z on pattern).

Take shoe fronts and placing one over the top of each sole (X on pattern to centre front) stitch all round the outside edge, working up and down through edge of soles and fronts, to join them together. Stuff very fully and firmly pushing the kapok in with an orange stick (6). Take the shoe backs and wrap them round the back of feet (with Y on pattern to centre back of sole). Stab stitch them to soles in the same way as the fronts, then catch the two points I on pattern together at centre fronts of feet and stitch shoes to socks working all round top edge of shoe (7).

Make the shoe laces by tying a small bow of thick black stranded cotton at the top centre front of each shoe, stitching several times through the knot to prevent it coming undone. Smear adhesive very thinly all round socks where the narrowest part of the trouser legs will come (Z on pattern). Slip a grey trouser leg over the top of each leg wire and pull down so that they have the appearance of being rather too short and there is a small piece of white sock showing. Press trousers well to legs all round at this position and when dry stuff the top part of trouser legs very fully and firmly. Do not forget to make sure that the trouser seams are at the *sides* of legs and that you have made a pair.

Assembling Place the head in the centre of the join between the two blue sections of body ball, over the opening. With a long needle and strong doubled thread stitch head to body, working several times round in a circle about 4 cm (1½ in) diameter so as to give a really thick neck.

Measure 2·5 cm (1 in) from where head joins body along the seam at each side of neck. Mark this position with a pin. Push the points of your scissors into the body a little lower down and just to one side of the seam, making a small hole. Pin the arms in place with the thumbs forwards and the centre top of sleeves at the position already marked, pushing the protruding pipe-cleaners into body through the hole. Stitch invisibly all round, starting underneath at the sleeve and body seams which should match. Leave the arms extended at right angles to the body for the present, but make sure there is not too much stuffing in their tops for they must eventually be bent down.

Place the legs together with the longer sides of the trousers on the outside. Join the inside leg seams by invisible stitching from top downwards about 3·5 cm (1½ in). Position the legs against lower half of body and pierce two holes so that the protruding leg wires can be pushed into the body. Pin the legs in place, matching side seams on trousers with side seams on body and stitch firmly in place, working several times all round the top of each one and adding any necessary extra stuffing as you work so that they are very firm. Catch the heels together with several strong stitches so that the toes are turned out at an exaggerated angle.

Embroider the twins' names on the left-hand side of the collars, using two strands of black embroidery cotton and bold straight stitches. Make sure that the 'DUM' and 'DEE' show from the front and that 'TWEEDLE' stretches round the back. Back the collars with iron-on interfacing and place one round each neck, keeping them in place with a little adhesive. Stitch two small loops of red ribbon to centre fronts for ties. Sew nine tiny pearl buttons to the front of each twin, looking at accompanying photograph for positions. If such small buttons are not available, cut tiny circles of white felt or plastic and stick them in place.

Snap-Fasteners The twins are attached to each other and to a board with snap-fasteners so that they can change places, putting the opposite arm round each other's neck, or stand separately with their arms at their sides. Because their bodies are soft any snap-fasteners sewn directly on to them would be difficult to press together – they therefore need a firm backing. To make such a backing cut a circle of card about 2 cm (¾ in) in diameter. Cut a circle of coloured felt a little larger than the card, to match the part of the toy to which the fastener is to be sewn. Gather round the edge of the felt, place the card in the centre (Fig. 4(1)) pull up gathers and secure by criss-cross stitches at the back (2). Sew the snap-fastener to the right side of the covered circle, working right through the card (3), then sew the covered circle to the toy and stitch several times round edge (4).

Back both halves of a large snap-fastener, using blue felt, then sew one half to each twin at side of body just under the arm to join the boys together side by side. Now back and sew another fastener, one half each to the other sides of their bodies so that when they change places they can still be attached together. Take the four remaining halves of

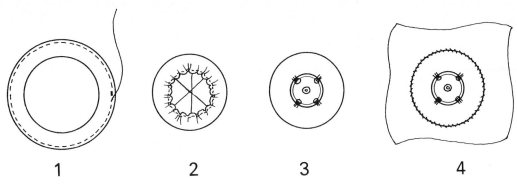

Fig. 4 Backing the snap-fasteners

the snap-fastener already sewn to the hands of both twins and back two with blue felt and two with grey. Place one arm from each figure round the other's neck and sew a blue-backed fastener to one shoulder of each boy so that the hand from his twin can snap on to it. Bend the outside arm of each twin straight down and sew a grey-backed fastener to each outside trouser seam so that a hand can be attached to each one. Now take four more medium-sized snap-fasteners and back only the halves similar to those you have just sewn on to the shoulders and trousers, two with grey and two with blue felt. Discard the other four halves which will not be used. Make the twins change places then sew a snap-fastener to their other shoulders and legs so that their hands can be fastened round each other's neck and to their sides when in this position.

Board Base Find a piece of firm board through which it is possible to push a needle, and large enough for the twins to stand on. Cut a piece of strong, green material to cover it which is a little larger all round, put one or two dabs of adhesive on the board and place the material over it with the edges overlapping (the adhesive is used instead of pins to hold the material while you work). Stand the twins on the material and make pencil marks at the positions of the snap-fasteners sewn to the soles of their shoes. Remove the twins and sew the corresponding halves of these

fasteners (which you have previously put on one side) to the base, working right through the material and the cardboard with very strong thread. Cut a second piece of cardboard the same size as the first but very much stronger and thicker. Stick this to the back of the first piece of card then fold the edges of the material round to the back and stick, making neat mitred corners, and finish off by sticking an odd piece of felt or strong paper over this to cover the wrong side completely.

The twins can now be snapped to each other and to their green base and their positions changed at will.

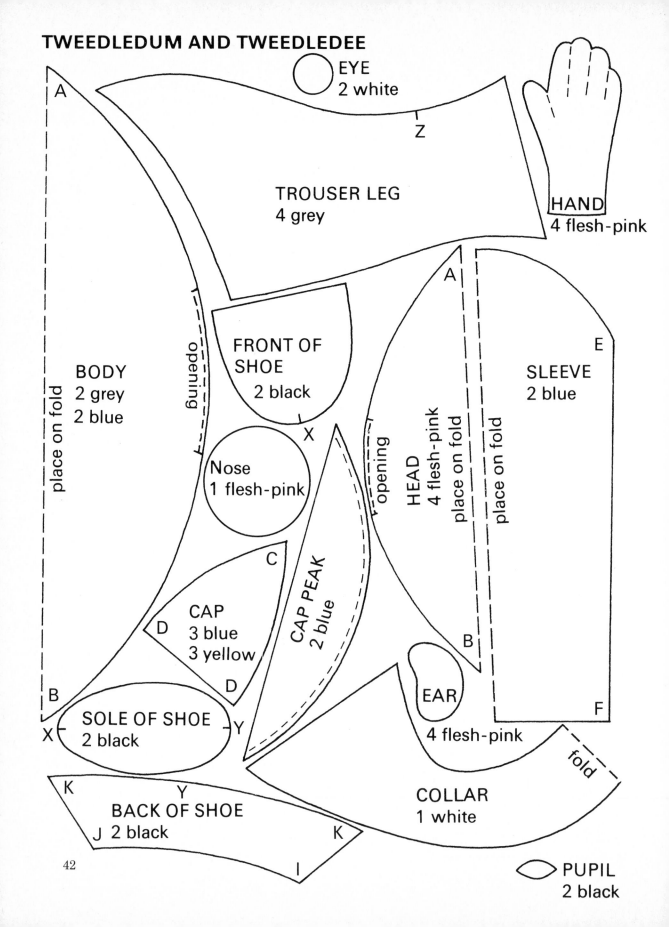

TWEEDLEDUM AND TWEEDLEDEE

EYE
2 white

HAND
4 flesh-pink

TROUSER LEG
4 grey

A
Z
A
E
SLEEVE
2 blue

opening

BODY
2 grey
2 blue

place on fold

FRONT OF
SHOE
2 black

place on fold

place on fold

opening

HEAD
4 flesh-pink

X

Nose
1 flesh-pink

C

B

CAP
3 blue
3 yellow

D

D

CAP PEAK
2 blue

B

F

EAR

4 flesh-pink

B

X

SOLE OF SHOE
2 black

Y

K

Y

BACK OF SHOE
J 2 black

fold

COLLAR
1 white

K

42

I

PUPIL
2 black

THE QUEEN OF HEARTS

A standing felt toy
Height: 37 cm (14½ in)

'The Queen fumed crimson with fury, and, after glaring at [Alice] for a moment like a wild beast, screamed "Off with her head!"'

The Queen stands firmly on a large flat base. Plans and suggestions are given for decorating her skirt but you should feel at liberty to experiment and use whatever materials are readily available.

MATERIALS
Saxe-blue (light blue with a greyish tinge) felt for bodice and skirt:
23 cm × 90 cm (9 in × 36 in)
Scraps of white felt for collar and cuffs
Yellow felt for crown:
23 cm × 30 cm (9 in × 12 in)
Strip of black felt for head-dress:
4 cm × 26 cm (1½ in × 10 in)
Scraps of red felt for mouth, shoe, fan and heart decorations
Flesh-pink felt for head and hands:
23 cm × 23 cm (9 in × 9 in)
White gauzy material for veil:
16 cm × 30 cm (6 in × 12 in)
Card and orange sticks
Red sequins and beads
Red, black, white and yellow braid ⎫ for
An odd piece of white fur fabric ⎬ trimming
Scraps of bright, striped material ⎭
Grey wool for hair
Wire for stiffening: 107 cm (42 in) long
Rag and adhesive tape for binding wire

Ten pipe-cleaners for stiffening fingers
Stout cardboard for stiffening head-dress and base
A gold filigree button for brooch
Six small pearls for ear-rings
Iron-on interfacing for stiffening
Kapok for stuffing: about 225 g (8 oz)
Adhesive

METHOD
Cut out the pieces as given on pages 52–55 (37 pieces). Make up the pieces separately and place on one side as finished. Russia braid was used to trim the cuffs, crown and fan, and was also used together with other braids and trimmings on the collar and skirt. You may prefer to substitute whatever trimmings you have already or to decorate the skirt with embroidery. In this case a pack of cards would serve as a guide for colours and designs.

Bodice and Arms On the wrong side join the side seams A-B. Turn right side out.

Collar Decorate both ends and one edge by sticking on braid, then turn raw ends neatly to the back. (Red Russia braid, yellow lampshade trimming and a small piece of black gimp were used for original.)

43

Cuffs Make two alike. On the longer half stitch red Russia braid along pointed edge as shown on pattern, leaving ends raw. Now sew braid to the other pointed edge but on the opposite side of work. (This is because this section of the cuff will eventually be turned back and the braid will then show.) Oversew seam C-D on the opposite side of work to the braid, turn right way out. Now oversew seam C-E on the wrong side to the braid on that section and turn that part of the cuff back (Fig. 1(3)). (The raw edges of braid will be secured and neatened in the seams.)

Crown Take one of the pieces and back it with iron-on interfacing. Stitch red and white Russia braid, red felt hearts and red sequins and beads in place as shown on pattern, turning the raw ends of braids to the back. Spread adhesive sparingly over the interfacing and stick this decorated piece to the plain piece, pressing the two firmly together.

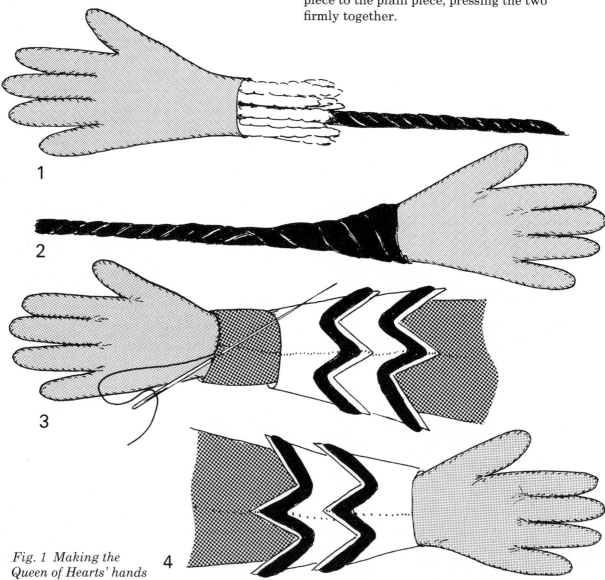

Fig. 1 Making the Queen of Hearts' hands

Fan Stick a felt piece to each card piece. Stitch a red sequin with a bead in the centre to the bottom point of each heart, working right through the card. Take two orange sticks (one is not strong enough) and stick them side by side to the card side of one of the hearts, half on the card and half protruding at the point for the handle (see broken lines on Fig. 2). Now stick the two hearts together, card side inside and with the top half of the sticks secured between the two hearts. Stick red Russia braid all round the edge of the fan, thus covering the join between the two hearts, starting on the sticks and working up one side, across top and down the other side on to the sticks. Smear adhesive on to sticks then roll a strip of red felt round them, stitching this neatly across base then up the length of the sticks and joining the felt at the top of the handle to the base of the fan.

Skirt Base Using strong button thread doubled, run a gathering thread all round outside edge of felt piece, place the cardboard piece on top of this, pull up gathers and secure the felt firmly by taking long, tight, criss-cross stitches across the *wrong* side of the card (Fig. 3). It is important to make sure your cardboard is really strong and will not bend – if necessary stick two or three thicknesses together to achieve this.

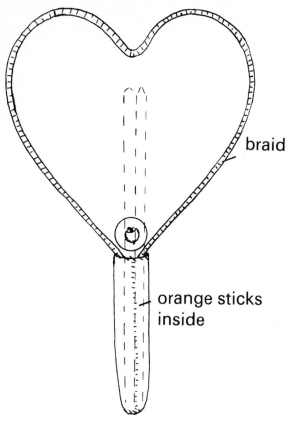

braid

orange sticks
inside

Fig. 2 The fan

of yellow felt and sew on red and white braids leaving raw ends to be covered later by fur.

Next cut out eighteen red felt hearts and stick in place. Pin a patch of red and white striped cotton material in place, turning in and hemming only the edge nearest the design you have just made. Turn the bottom edge to back of work and tack. Tack round rest of patch leaving edges raw – they will eventually be hidden under braid and fur. Sew white Russia braid down hemmed edge of patch. Press work on wrong side.

On right side neatly oversew lower half on centre back seam Z-Y keeping it as flat as possible. Tack a patch of bright, striped cotton material across back of skirt covering the seam, placing it so that the top raw edge will eventually be covered by the fur and the sides by braid. Turn the lower edge to the back of work. (For the original, grey and white striped cotton material were used with strips of red Russia braid stitched across it for added colour.) Stitch wide red and white braid down both edges thus covering the raw edges between the three patches, turning bottom raw end to back of work and leaving top end raw where it will eventually be covered by fur.

Skirt Back the piece with iron-on interfacing then decorate it, sticking the felt pieces and stitching the braid in place. You will save a lot of unnecessary sewing by working as follows, using pattern as a guide, and turning any raw ends which come at top or bottom of skirt to the back of work.

Stitch braid down centre front. On both sides of this centre point stick yellow and black felt semi-circles and stitch red and white braid round them. Sew on semi-circles of white, black yellow and red braid leaving ends raw where they will eventually be covered by other materials. Now attach strip of red and white braid, sew black and white braids round it, leaving ends raw. Stick on triangular piece

Head-dress Cut two strips of very strong card 2 cm × 13 cm ($\frac{3}{4}$ in × 5 in) (if necessary stick two thicknesses together). Place these pieces together end to end and stick a piece of red braid along one edge thus joining them into one long strip, taking care to attach the braid only at the extreme edge (Fig. 4(1)). Turn the raw ends to the back. Take the strip of black felt which you cut for the head-dress, smear one side of it with adhesive then stick it to the card piece so that the braid shows along one edge. Fold the felt round the opposite edge and stick it to the other side of card. Stick a piece of black braid along the front edge (2). The head-dress will fold in the centre to form a point where the two strips of card meet end to end inside the felt (3).

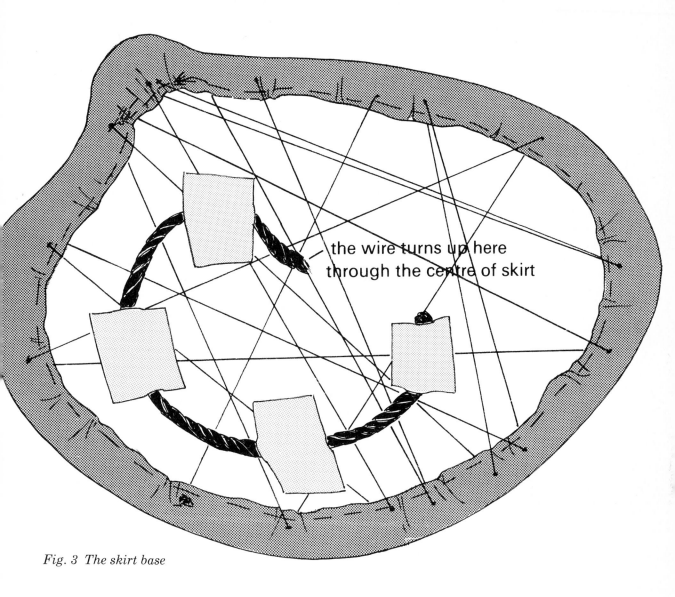

the wire turns up here
through the centre of skirt

Fig. 3 The skirt base

47

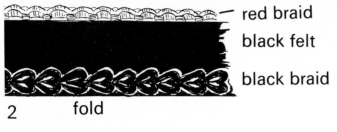

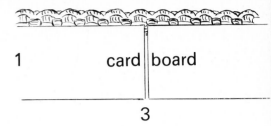

red braid

black felt

black braid

2 fold

1 card board

3

Fig. 4 The head-dress

Shoe Smear a little adhesive round the edge of one side of the card piece (the inner sole) and place it sticky side up on top of the larger felt piece (the upper) as in Fig. 5(1). Fold the superfluous felt on the upper round on to the card and press in place (2). Stick the smaller felt piece (the outer sole) over the card to neaten (3). Turn right way up and stuff firmly (4).

Hands Cut between the fingers as shown by broken lines on pattern, then oversew very neatly all round the outside edge, except for the short, straight wrist end. Push a doubled pipe-cleaner into each finger as for the White Rabbit (page 15). Cut 28 cm (11 in) wire and bind with adhesive tape. Push one end into the hand among the pipe-cleaners (Fig. 1(1)). Stuff the hand, pushing a little kapok into each finger and shaping it well then bind over cleaners and on to edge of the hand with adhesive tape.*(2) Push the wire into sleeve of bodice, having first slipped the cuff loosely on to sleeve, turning the spare wire at right angles at centre of bodice so that it protrudes at waist edge. Arrange hand with thumb to front and underarm sleeve at centre of palm side. Stitch sleeve to arm all round wrist, gathering it in to fit (3). Smear a little adhesive round edge of sleeve. Pull down cuff, matching its seam with that on the sleeve and press it well to sleeve until dry (4). Make the other hand and insert into other sleeve in the same way.

Head Place the pieces together and on the wrong side join them C-S-D- and E-F. Insert head gusset, stitching on both sides C-G, then join the two head pieces together G-H. Turn right side out, pushing the top of the head carefully down through the neck with the knob end of a knitting needle. Fold the mouth lining in half across broken line

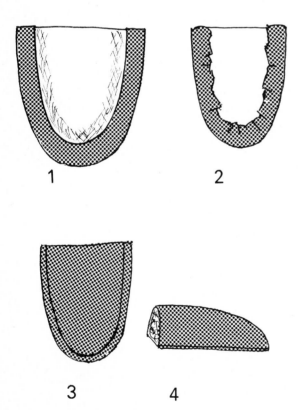

1   **2**

3   **4**

Fig. 5 Making the shoe

Right *The Queen of Hearts*

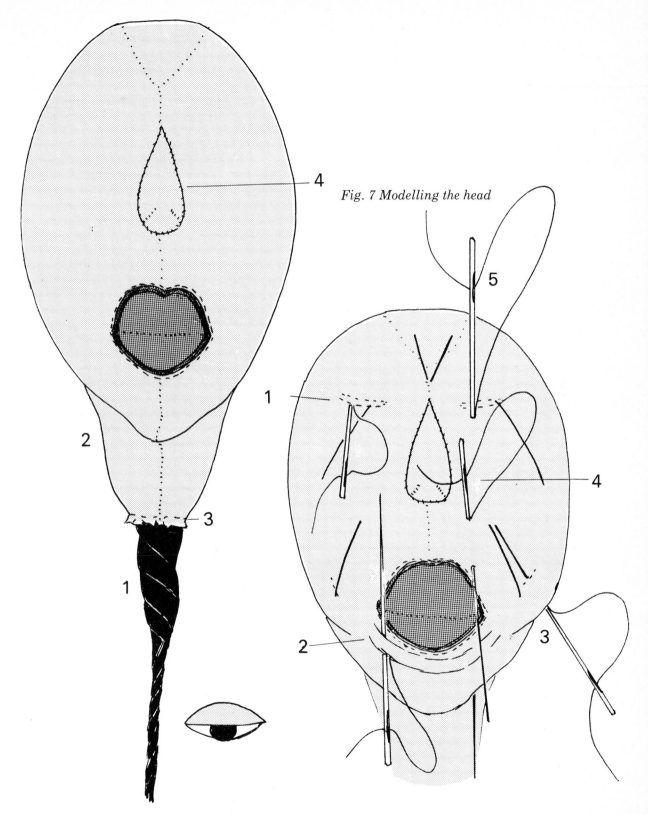

Fig. 7 Modelling the head

Fig. 6 Attaching the head

49

Left *The Red Queen*

X-X and stitch close to the fold on the wrong side thus making a small tuck. Using red sewing thread insert mouth lining into hole in head, carefully matching letters and stab stitching on the right side working all round X-D-X-E-X. Using a blunt orange stick or knitting needle carefully push out all the points on head, nose, lips, chin, etc., then stuff the head very firmly, pushing the kapok into all the corners and points.

Cut 51 cm (20 in) of wire and bind tightly with adhesive tape. Bind one end with several thicknesses of rag for about 13 cm (5 in) and push this end up into head (Fig. 6(1). Make sure head is *very* firmly stuffed and as you work press it out sideways. Stuff the neck very firmly (2), then stitch edge of neck to rag binding the wire (3). Take the nose piece and very neatly join the little darts as shown by broken lines on pattern (which will be under the nostrils) by oversewing on the wrong side. Stitch the nose to head over the pointed piece S on pattern (4), poking a little stuffing in as you work, so as to make it very pointed and tip-tilted. To make folds and add expression to the face, take a long, slim needle and doubled thread which exactly matches the face and sew a few stitches from where the eyes will be (level with bridge of nose) right through to back of head, pulling them very tightly to make eye sockets (Fig. 7(1)). Make a fold under lower lip by stitching up and down taking a large tuck in the felt (2). Make a big fold at each side of face (3). Pucker the face above mouth by taking a tight stitch each side (4). Using strong button thread take a few stitches from each eye socket to deep under chin (almost on the neck) to push out entire front of face and sink the eyes even more (5). The back of head will be covered with strange dents and dimples, but this will not show on the finished toy. With flesh-coloured thread embroider two straight lines from eye socket to top of cheek and two more lower on face for folds. Now stick on lips, covering the stitching all round

mouth. Stick on nostrils. Glue white eyes in place so that they completely fill sockets. Stick a black pupil to centre lower part of each, then pink lids across top. Embroider two black frown lines at centre forehead, using one strand of thread. Colour the nose, cheeks, chin and centre forehead pink (see face tinting of Tweedledum and Tweedledee page 38). With short lines of stitches make three red wrinkles in the outer corner of each eye. Place on one side to dry thoroughly, preferably overnight. Finally, embroider grey, bushy eyebrows and a kiss-curl at each side of face.

Assembling Working up through the open waist of bodice stuff both arms, thoroughly embedding the wires so that they cannot be felt from the outside, but not making the arms so full that it will not be possible to bend them later. Cut small slit at centre top of bodice where shown by XXXX on pattern, push the long wire protruding from head down through this slit and ease the neck right down inside bodice. Stitch bodice to head all round neck as high up under chin as possible. Turn back the bodice and twist the ends of the two arm wires round and round the neck wire from the point where they all meet in centre of bodice downwards. Bind the three twisted thicknesses together with adhesive tape (you will still have a length of single bound wire at the end). Stuff the bodice very firmly indeed, working from both front and back so that the wires are well embedded. Slip the skirt up over the wire (which will still protrude from the bottom) and pin it in place as high up as possible under the arms, making sure the centre strip of red braid on skirt comes at centre front of bodice and the back opening of skirt at centre back of bodice. Stitch firmly in place working all round waist. Leave slit in back of skirt open. Bend end of protruding wire at right angles exactly at skirt hem line. Fold skirt back. Curl wire round in a flat semi-circle and fix this to inside of skirt base with small pieces of adhesive tape (Fig. 3), making sure you match X on base with centre front of skirt and Y with centre back.

Pin skirt to base all round edge and using strong doubled thread, oversew firmly in place except for the short section across foot position shown on pattern. Leave this open. Smear a little adhesive on this protruding foot position, then push foot just under skirt and stitch skirt firmly across top of foot. The finished appearance will be of the toe of one red shoe just showing under the side of skirt. Stuff skirt very full and firmly indeed using a long stuffing stick to make sure there is no ugly dented ridge round the base, but that the skirt sweeps smoothly to the ground. It is best to use kapok for this but as you work on you can use up cuttings and snippings to help fill the skirt. The Queen has a smooth straight front but a very pronounced bustle-type behind. When you are quite sure the skirt is absolutely full, sew up the back opening (this will eventually be covered by fur). Cut a piece of white fur fabric to the shape and size shown on the pattern (remembering that only half the piece is shown), but make it about 1 cm ($\frac{1}{2}$ in) larger all round. Turn back this spare 1 cm ($\frac{1}{2}$ in) and stick. Make ermine tails with black stitches in wool or by painting with black ink. When dry stick the fur to back of skirt from waist downwards.

Stick a piece of red Russia braid down centre front of bodice, and a piece of black braid round waist for a belt. The edges can be left raw at centre front as they will be covered later. The general effect of the belt is of being a little higher at the front than the back, giving the Queen a rather paunchy appearance. Remove any tacking threads still showing on patches on skirt and stick Russia braid all round the base going over the top of the shoe, thus covering your stitches. Make the join at centre back, oversewing it neatly with red thread.

The Hair Smear the back of the head with adhesive, working from the top to the base of neck and across a little wider than the head gusset. Cover this with strands of grey wool working up and down and allowing the ball of wool to unwind as you work and pressing it into the adhesive. The object of this is just to cover the unsightly stitches and bumps on the back of the head. Now take a bundle of thick wool about 30 cm (12 in) long (about 40 strands), lay this across top of head and secure with several long stitches in flesh-coloured cotton for a centre parting (about 2·5 cm (1 in) long).

Lift hair and smear adhesive down each side of head, then press wool down at each side of face, arranging the strands neatly. At the same time stick on ears immediately below kiss-curls so that they just show below hair. (Leave the bottom lobes free to take the ear-rings later.) Note that the hair will cover the ends of eyebrows. Gather the wool into the nape of neck and tie in a short pony-tail. Twist up into a little bun and using a long needle and matching grey wool, stitch firmly in this position, tucking all the loose ends under as you work and securing the bun to head. (It will rest on back of bodice.)

Finishing off Place the collar round the Queen's neck, braid side outside, tucking it under her bun at the back and crossing it and stitching in place at centre front over belt. Sew a gilt filigree button to centre of collar where it crosses and stick a little red felt shape to centre of button for a jewel. The button is her brooch.

Gather along one of the long edges of the veil, pull up to 11·5 cm ($4\frac{1}{2}$ in). Fasten off. Pin veil to Queen's head arranging gathers evenly. Start at back end of centre parting and pin gathers round at an even distance of about 2·5 cm (1 in) from front edge of hair. Oversew the veil firmly to head using white thread and working over gathered edge. Snip off back corners of veil to round off edges. Using strong, red thread doubled and a long needle, stitch on crown, working all round the red Russia braid on inner edge in a long backstitch. Attach the crown all along gathers on veil, then curl the remainder at each side forwards to a position under the ear. Thread three small pearls or similar beads together for each ear-ring and sew one to the lobe of each ear. Try on head-dress, looking at the Tenniel illustration for correct position then stick it in place to each side of top of head, red braid towards the back. Pull the left arm forward and arrange the hand with the forefinger pointing forwards. Turn the right arm upwards from elbow and put the fan into the Queen's hand, closing her fingers tightly round the handle.

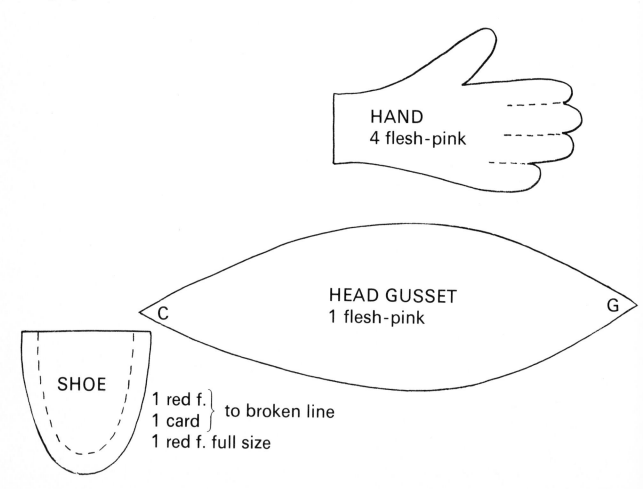

HAND
4 flesh-pink

HEAD GUSSET
1 flesh-pink

C

G

SHOE

1 red f.
1 card
} to broken line
1 red f. full size

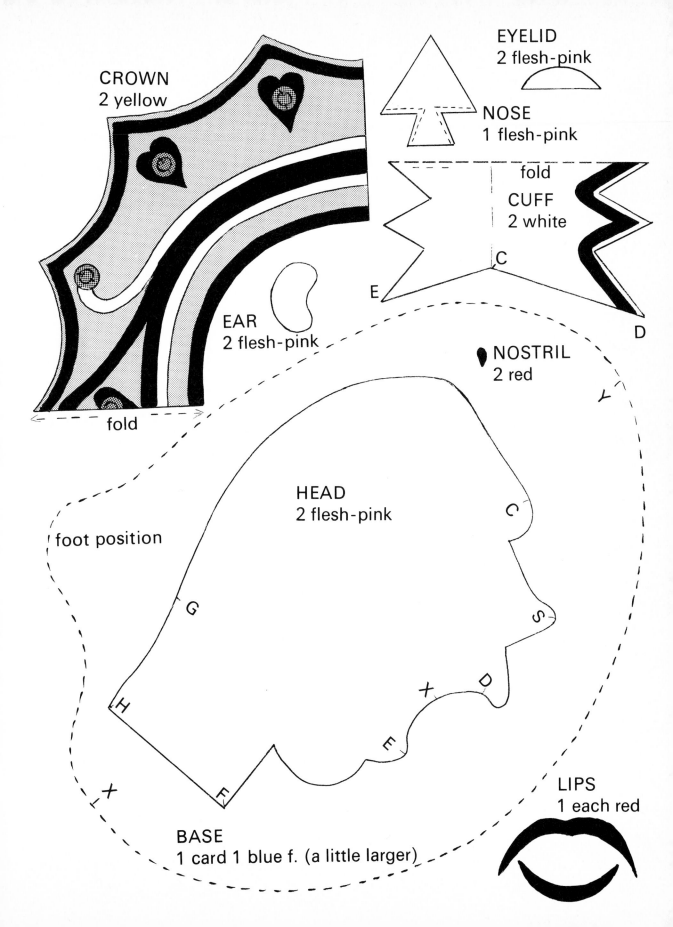

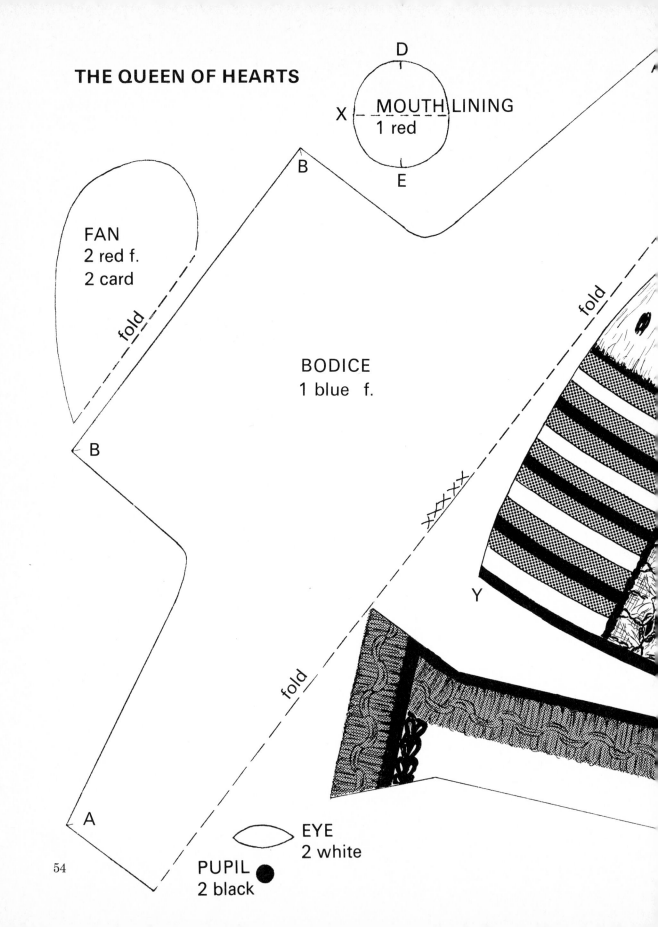

THE QUEEN OF HEARTS

D

X — MOUTH LINING
1 red

E

FAN
2 red f.
2 card

fold

B

B

BODICE
1 blue f.

fold

fold

Y

A

fold

EYE
2 white

PUPIL
2 black

54

SKIRT
1 blue

place on fold

COLLAR
1 white

fold

55

THE ROCKING-HORSE-FLY

A felt model mounted on wire rockers
Height: 26 cm (10 in)

'. . . half way up that bush, you'll see a Rocking-horse-fly, if you look. It's made entirely of wood, and gets about by swinging itself from branch to branch.'

MATERIALS

White felt for wings and eyes:
15 cm × 23 cm (6 in × 9 in)
Yellow felt for all other parts:
23 cm × 30 cm (9 in × 12 in)
Red felt for spots, nostrils and ear linings
Scraps of black felt for eyes
Red Russia braid for bridle:
about $11\frac{1}{2}$ cm ($4\frac{1}{2}$ in)
Red wool for mane
Cardboard for stiffening (a cereal box would be suitable)
Wire for legs and rockers:
approximately 0·25 cm ($\frac{1}{10}$ in) diameter, 2·75 metres (3 yards) long
A little brown paint or enamel for colouring wire (a spray can would be helpful)
Multi-core solder for joining wire
Kapok for stuffing
Adhesive
Adhesive tape

Optional Scraps of green felt and plastic-covered gardening wire for ivy

METHOD

Cut out the pieces of card and felt as indicated on page 60 (33 pieces). Then place the 15 card pieces – body cube pieces, front, base, sides and back of neck, front and base

of body and sides of head – on to yellow felt, pencil round each one and cut out a piece for each about 0·5 cm ($\frac{1}{4}$ in) larger all round than the pencil markings (48 pieces in all).

Rockers and Legs Cut two pieces of wire each 48 cm (19 in) long for rockers (Fig. 1(1)).
Then cut a piece 53 cm (21 in) long for a support. Using pliers bend this piece to a rectangle (2) having each short end 6·5 cm ($2\frac{1}{2}$ in) and each long side 20 cm (8 in) long, with the join in the centre of one long side. Ask someone to hold the pieces together with the pliers in the flame of a blowtorch, camping or kitchen gas stove to heat them while you quickly run a little multi-core solder between the wires to join them here and there. (This is a simple matter even for someone with no sense of mechanics!) When cold bend the rockers to the shape shown in the diagram.
Cut 63.5 cm (25 in) of wire for the back legs (3) and 56 cm (22 in) for the front legs (4). Bend these to the shape shown, each pair in one long piece passing through the body from side to side. The straight piece at the centre of the back legs 2·5 cm (1 in) wide will be hidden in the body and on the front legs, where it should be 4 cm ($1\frac{1}{2}$ in) wide, it will be hidden in the body cube. Solder these two pairs of legs to rockers at (5) and

(6) in Fig. 1. Now solder about 2·5 cm (1 in) of wire at right angles across the straight centre piece of wire which will be hidden inside body – on both pairs of legs (7). This is to steady the wire inside the toy and prevent it swivelling and slipping. Paint all the wire parts brown and leave to dry thoroughly. The rockers and legs are meant to be twigs so bends and bumps, lumps of paint or any irregularities only add to the realistic appearance.

Wings Lightly pencil the veins on to the four white felt wings, remembering to reverse two of them so as to make two pairs. Using one strand of black cotton, embroider over the pencil markings taking a series of straight stitches about 0·5 cm ($\frac{1}{4}$ in) long. Stick the felt wings together with a card piece between each pair.

Spots Cut out twenty-eight spots in red felt and following the pattern, arrange them on the appropriate pieces. Make sure that the pencil marks are now on the back of the felt pieces but use these as a guide to the eventual shape of the parts. Place *five* spots on two of the square body pieces (9) and *one* on one of the others (10), leaving the other three plain; *three* on each of the two body sides (11); *five* on each of the two neck pieces (12); *one* on the front of the neck (13). Keep them all in position with a tiny dab of adhesive, then sew in place, stab stitching all round the edge of each spot.

Stiffening the pieces Take all the card pieces except those for the head and with a scant smear of adhesive fix each one on the back of the matching felt piece, using the pencil marks as a guide (Fig. 2(1)). Turn the

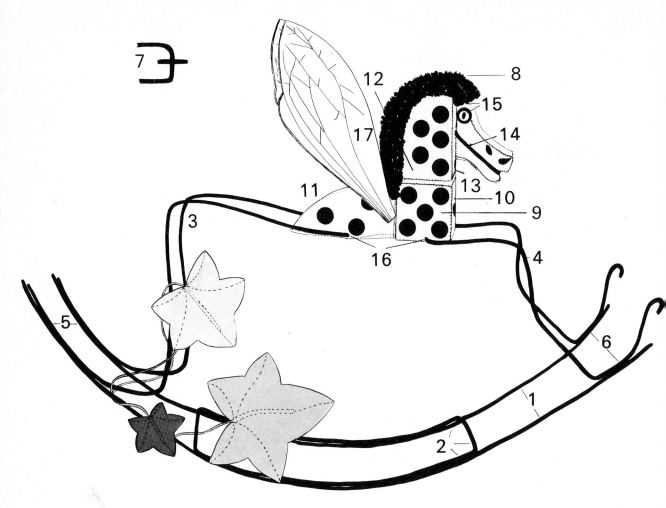

Fig. 1 The Rocking-Horse-Fly

spare felt all round the edge to the back and tack in place (2), stitching through the felt only – not the card (3).

Body Cube Make the six square pieces into a cube by oversewing the edges together on the right side using doubled thread that exactly matches the felt. Have a piece with five spots on each side, the piece with one spot in the front and a plain piece at top, bottom and back. Attach the bottom piece by the back edge only (to allow for inserting legs later). Stuff the cube firmly, but leave the base open.

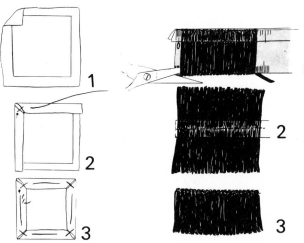

Fig. 2 Stiffening the pieces Fig. 3 The mane

Main Body Take the two pieces for the sides of the body (these are unbacked) and on the wrong side join darts A-B, then join these two pieces together C-A-D. Turn right side out. Insert stiffened front of body, matching letters and oversewing all round E-C-E on the right side. Insert base of body, oversewing on the right side F-E-E-F. Leave the rest open for fitting legs later but stuff firmly.

Neck On the right side join the front of the neck to the side neck pieces, oversewing on the right side G-H. Join on the back of neck I-G-G-I. Stuff very firmly then oversew base of neck in place H-I-I-H-H.

Head Stick the two card pieces to the felt pieces, reversing one so as to make a pair. Cut a strip of yellow felt 1·5 cm ($\frac{1}{2}$ in) wide and long enough to fit all round the edge of the head. Oversew the strip to one side of head, working on the right side from J all round to the same point again. Oversew the two short ends of the strip together. Then attach the other side of the head in the same way, stuffing it firmly just before completing the stitching. Following the pattern, stick red braid in place (Fig. 1(14)) folding the raw ends round to the back of head. Cut out two red nostrils and two little oval red spots and stick one of each to each side of head.

Assembling Body Stick the head to the front of neck and the base of neck to the top of the body cube, reinforcing these with a few stitches taken with a long needle. Stick the front of the main body to the back of the body cube and strengthen this with a few stitches.

Mane Wind red wool round a ruler until 11·5 cm ($4\frac{1}{2}$ in) are well covered with five or six layers. Stick a piece of narrow transparent adhesive tape over one edge of the ruler and cut wool along the other edge (Fig. 3(1)). Machine or backstitch down the centre of the adhesive tape (2), then pull this off and discard. Fold the wool in half and stitch right through the double thickness (3). Stick mane from top of head all down neck, then clip short (Fig. 1(8)).

Ears and Eyes Stick each red ear lining to a yellow ear. Gather in the base of the now completed ears and stitch one to each side of head. Cut out the eyes. Stick each white circle to a black one then stick a black oval to the centre of each and glue the completed eyes one to each side of head (Fig. 1(15)).

Attaching the Rockers and Legs Slip the straight piece at top of front legs inside the body cube, push in any extra stuffing needed and finish oversewing the square at the base of this cube. Insert the back legs into the main body piece in the same way, stuff and finish oversewing the base in position (16). The toy should now be very firm and rock easily. Stick the wings in position, one to each side of body (17).

Optional If you want to make some ivy leaves to twine round your insect as in the Tenniel illustration, pick a few real leaves of varying size and use them as a pattern to cut out pairs of felt leaves in two or three shades of green. Stick these together in pairs, first pushing a piece of green plastic-covered garden wire between them for a stalk. Stab stitch down both sides of the enclosed wire for the centre vein, then work rows of stab stitching to indicate other veins. Make as many or as few of these as you wish and twist them round the legs and rockers.

THE ROCKING-HORSE FLY

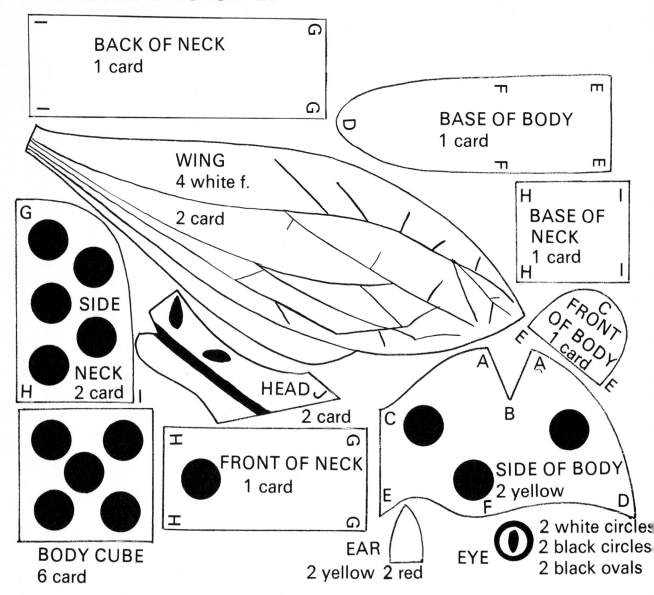

BACK OF NECK
1 card

G

G

BASE OF BODY
1 card

D

F

E

F

E

WING
4 white f.

2 card

BASE OF
NECK
1 card

H

I

H

I

G

SIDE

NECK
2 card

H

I

FRONT
OF BODY
1 card

C

E

E

A

A

B

HEAD

2 card

C

SIDE OF BODY
2 yellow

B

D

E

F

BODY CUBE
6 card

FRONT OF NECK
1 card

H

G

H

G

EAR
2 yellow 2 red

EYE

2 white circles
2 black circles
2 black ovals

THE RED QUEEN

A standing felt toy
Height: 35 cm (14 in)

'Where do you come from?', said the Red Queen, 'And where are you going? Look up, speak nicely and don't twiddle your fingers all the time.'

MATERIALS

Red felt for all parts:
34 cm × 90 cm (13½ in × 36 in)
Red Russia braid for trimming:
about 1·2 metres (1⅓ yards)
*One large red bead for top of crown (or a small wooden ball sold for making dolls' heads, painted red)
Smaller beads and sequins for decorating crown
*Red netting for snood: 11 cm × 20 cm (4½ in × 8 in) (perhaps part of a plastic net bag sold containing fruit or nuts)
Red braid for edging snood:
about 16 cm (6½ in)
Scraps of black and white felt for eyes
*Red wool for hair
*Fine red jersey-type material suitable for draping for shawl:
20 cm × 33 cm (8 in × 13 in)
(dyed underwear material may be used)
*18 cm (7 in) broken knitting needle,
gauge 3¼ mm (US size 3) for sceptre
*A scrap of iron-on interfacing material for crown
*Two packets of pipe-cleaners for stiffening felt rolls, fingers, etc.
A shoe box or cardboard of similar thickness
Some pieces of thick material such as an old blanket or towel
} for making the rings

*Wire for foundation
*Kapok for stuffing
*Adhesive
*Adhesive tape

METHOD

Cut out the pieces as given on pages 68–69 (51 pieces), the hands as given for Queen of Hearts on page 52 (4 pieces) and two strips 3·5 cm × 10 cm (1½ in × 4 in) for the elbow puffs (57 pieces in all). Use red felt for all the pieces except the eyes and pupils.

Skirt Stitch two rows of red Russia braid round the edge of the circle as shown on pattern.

Crown Back one of the pieces with iron-on interfacing then decorate it with red beads and sequins as in Fig. 1. Stick this decorated piece to the plain piece. Fold the crown round matching X's and stick in place by smearing a little adhesive over the extending tab, which will be on the inside.

Make a felt roll to fit round crown using two thicknesses of pipe-cleaner (see Fig. 1). Stitch this invisibly to the crown all round the lower edge, having the seam on the roll towards the inside where it will not show and the join at the centre back to

61

match the position of the join on the crown.

Take the card centre for crown, cut a rough circle of red felt about 2 cm (¾ in) larger all round and stick the card circle to the centre of the felt circle. Fold a pipe-cleaner in half, smear the fold with adhesive and push it into the hole in the ball (Fig. 2(1)). Make a small hole in the middle of the centre of card and felt, push the ends of pipe-cleaner through (2), twist round on wrong side and stick to card with small pieces of adhesive tape (3). If your ball has a hole right through it so that the pipe-cleaner shows at the top, touch the tip with red paint.

Fold the spare felt down all round the card circle as shown in Fig. 2 and slip the piece complete with ball up through the base until the felt folded downwards just shows between the points of the crown. Turn upside down and stick the spare felt on centre piece to inside of crown, pressing the folds well together until dry and set.

Hands and Arms Make up the hands as given for the Queen of Hearts, page 48, working as far as * but having 14 cm (5½ in) of wire for each arm. Be sure to keep the adhesive tape binding tight and slim, for this Queen has skinny little arms and if the binding is too bulky the narrow sleeves will not fit over them.

Take the sleeves and on the wrong side join the top darts A-B, then join underarm

Fig. 1 The Red Queen

63

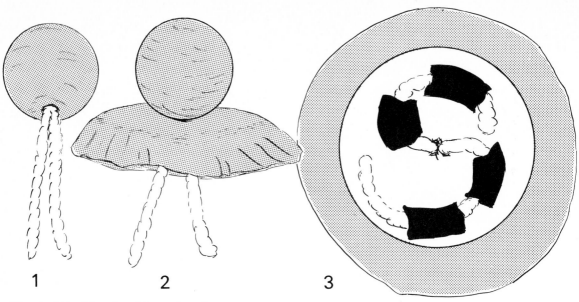

Fig. 2 Attaching bead to centre of crown

seams C-D. Carefully turn right way out. (A pair of slim, long-nosed pliers are a help in this job, for you can push them into the sleeve, grasp a fold of felt and easily pull it through.) Pull a sleeve well down on to each arm wire, having the seam at centre of palm and making sure you have a pair, i.e. thumbs on opposite sides. Stitch the sleeve to the hand working all round wrist. Cut a piece of felt which is just wide enough to cover two thicknesses of pipe-cleaner and stitch this together to make a felt roll to fit round wrist (Fig. 1(5)). Make two of these and stitch them invisibly in place, having the seam to the inside where it will not show and the join matching the sleeve seam. These rolls cover the join between sleeve and hand. Stuff the arms firmly so that the wires are completely embedded, but not so full that they will not bend.

Fig. 3 Sleeve puffs

Take the strips of felt for the elbow puffs and join each one into a ring by seaming the short ends together on the wrong side. Turn right way out. Run a gathering thread along both edges of one ring using a separate needle and thread for each and leaving these hanging, then slip the ring over the arm with lower edge 2 cm ($\frac{3}{4}$ in) from the wrist and matching the seam with that on the sleeve. Pull up the gathers to fit arm and stitch the puff in place, working all round both edges and using the needles and threads already attached (6). This puff covers the elbow. Make and attach the other one in the same way, testing to make sure the elbows will bend. Take the pieces for the top sleeve puffs and on the wrong side join the top darts E-F and the two side darts G-H. Turn right way out. You now have two little caps (look at Fig. 3 for side view). Sew a zigzag of red Russia braid to each one.

Rings Start with the top ring which will be almost hidden under the Queen's skirt. Stick each card circle to a circle of the thick padding material. (If you card is rather flimsy and is likely to bend, stick two thicknesses together.) Push the points of your scissors through the centre of both circles making a hole barely large enough to take a piece of wire bound with adhesive tape when you eventually assemble the parts. Gather all round the edge of both felt circles, place a padded card circle in the centre of each, padding towards the felt, pull up the gathers tightly and fasten off. Place the two circles together, gathers inside, and oversew them neatly together all round the edge. Sew red Russia braid round the edge thus covering the join between the two circles. Cut a very small cross in the centre of the red felt on both sides. Be sure it *is* small as it will stretch as you stuff through it. Using a blunt orange stick push tiny pieces of kapok at a time through the crossed slits and pad tightly to shape shown (Fig. 1(8)). The crossed slits will by now have become a small round hole. Now make the two small rings and the large ring in exactly the same way.

Head Place the two pieces together and on the wrong side join them J-K-L-X-M. Turn right side out and very carefully push out all the points of chin, nose, forehead, etc. Stuff very firmly indeed taking particular care over the above-mentioned points and pushing the head out sideways to give width to the cheeks. Cut and bind a piece of wire approximately 38 cm (15 in) long then push one end through the neck and well up into the head (see instructions for Queen of Hearts' head, page 50). Sew up back seam M-N neatly and invisibly, at the same time pushing in small pieces of kapok so that the neck is very firm and the wire completely embedded. Gather round open end of neck N-J-N, pull up to fit tightly round the wire and fasten off.

Body Place the two pieces together and on the wrong side join seams O-P-Q on both sides. Turn right side out. Take head and slip protruding wire into top of body through neck opening O-X-O, having the

centre front and centre back seams on neck at X. The wire will protrude at base of body. Stitch neck edge of body to stuffed neck of head working all round O-X-O-X-O. Stuff the body firmly, pushing out the shoulders well at P and completely embedding the wire. Gather all round the bottom open end Q-Q-Q, pull up to fit tightly round wire and fasten off, leaving wire protruding.

Features and Hair With a long, slim needle and strong thread sink the eye sockets by taking a stitch from the back of the head through to the front to each eye position and back again, pulling them tightly. Don't worry about unsightly dents on the back of head. Stick the whites of the eyes in place, pressing well in, then tiny black pupils. Stick red lids over these so that very little of each eye shows. With doubled thread that exactly matches the felt make the furrow lines on both sides of face by taking long stitches and pulling them tightly ((1) and (2) on Fig. 1). Then make three 'scowl' lines at centre of forehead (3). Using six strands of red embroidery cotton make a drooping mouth. Embroider brows with red wool. Smear a little adhesive round the head between broken lines on pattern and bind red wool round and round for the hair – rather like a bandage. (The point on back of head helps to shape and style the hair.) Take nine lengths of red wool about 66 cm (26 in) long. Knot them together at one end then plait them tightly and knot the other ends to stop plait unravelling. Using matching wool sew one end of the plait to the point on back of head then coil it round and round to make a high bun of hair, stitching it to the head as you work and tucking the end inside so that it is hidden. Do not worry about the gap on top of the head between the bun and wool bound round the forehead. This will eventually be covered by the crown.

Take the piece of red netting, find the centre of the long side and pin this to the centre back seam of the neck, just covering the hair and turning the cut edge under for about 1 cm ($\frac{1}{2}$ in). Stitch in place working on both sides from centre back (M on pattern) across bound wool to top of head (X on pattern). Fold and gather the net upwards to form a snood (Fig. 1(9)). Stitch in a little bunch to the top of the head where it will eventually be hidden by the crown. Cut two tiny scraps of felt to represent ear lobes and stick them in place, at the same time edging the snood by sticking or stitching a piece of red braid round the part which will eventually show. The crown will eventually hide the raw ends, but do not add this yet.

Assembling Make a small felt roll containing two pipe-cleaners to fit round the Queen's neck and stitch this invisibly in place (4). Slip the skirt upwards on to body, attach braid at centre back and stitch in place all round waist 4 cm (1$\frac{1}{2}$ in) below neck roll. Sew Russia braid in a zigzag pattern across the back from waist upwards for about 1·5 cm ($\frac{1}{2}$ in) (see Fig. 4), then sew a piece of similar braid all round the waist (Fig. 1(17)) having join at body seam on right where it will eventually be covered by the arm.

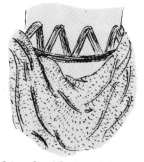

Fig. 4 Attaching braid at waist

Bend the wires protruding from tops of the arms inwards at a right angle. Push the points of your scissors into the Queen's body about 1·5 cm ($\frac{1}{2}$ in) below the shoulder points P, and slightly to one side of the side seam so as not to damage this. Make sure the arms are well stuffed right to the top, then push the wires into the holes, matching underarm seams with side seams on body and top darts to shoulder seams. Stitch each one in place, working several times all round open ends of arms. Take the top puffs and pin one over the top of each arm. Ladder stitch them in place, turning the raw edges under as you work (10). This is rather an awkward job, but a long, slim needle and pointed scissors to tuck the edges in are a help. Bend both arms upwards at right angles at the elbows.

Take the top ring and push pointed scissors right through the centre hole, twisting them several times to clear a passage. Smear a little adhesive over the base of the body, thread the ring on to the wire, push it up close against the body and hold it firmly there until the adhesive is dry and set. Thread first the large ring then one of the small ones in place in the same way and stick in position.

Cut a strip of red felt 3 cm (1$\frac{1}{4}$ in) wide and 22 cm (8$\frac{1}{2}$ in) long. Fold and stick the edges to the back, reducing the strip to about 1·5 cm ($\frac{1}{2}$ in) wide. Smear a little adhesive on to the wire just below the small ring and attach one end of this strip to it. Roll it round and round tightly and sew the end in place, arranging it to come at the back if possible. Ladder stitch the top of the felt roll to the underside of the small ring, working all round. Thread on and stick the second small ring in place, in the same way as the others (11). Ladder stitch the lower edge of felt roll to top of the second small ring (12). Take one of the last two large felt circles, run a gathering thread all round the edge but do not pull it up – leave the needle and thread hanging. Make a small hole in the centre. Smear a little adhesive over base of the last small ring on the wire, then thread the prepared felt circle on and leave until dry and set. Thread on the last circle of thick padding. Close beneath the felt padding, bend the protruding wire sharply at right angles, then twist it round in a flat spiral. Stick this spiral to one of the remaining large strong card circles with a lot of adhesive tape, tucking it into place with pointed scissors. Spread adhesive over the underside of the thick padding circle and press well down over the top of wire and adhesive tape. Pack plenty of kapok between padding and felt circle, then pull up gathers on felt, fastening them off securely on the underside of cardboard. The Queen should now stand quite firmly.

Take the last large felt and card circles, gather round the felt and pull over the card. Smear adhesive over the wrong side of this, turn the Queen upside down and stick it to the base to give a flat, neat finish. Oversew this to the base all round the edge then stitch a piece of Russia braid all round to cover stitches (13).

Stand the Queen on a table and arrange the skirt in a series of folds catching these invisibly together through the braid on extreme edge (14). About seven such folds will probably suffice (15).

Shawl Hang the jersey material over the Queen's right arm, drape it round the back in soft folds and tuck the other end under her left elbow (Fig. 1). Stitch the shawl here and there to the arms, skirt and back of the large ring wherever necessary to keep it firmly in an attractive position. Smear adhesive all round inside of crown and stick it to the head – noting the very forward, tilted position shown in Fig. 1.

Sceptre Cut a strip of felt as long as the piece of knitting needle and just wide enough to cover it when folded round. Smear this with adhesive and lay the needle on it. When dry, roll the felt round and oversew it in place across both ends and down its length. Lay the top 2 cm ($\frac{3}{4}$ in) on to the top piece of card and stick it in place. Smear a little adhesive over both sides of card and lay one felt piece on each side of it. Stab stitch the two felt pieces together all round the outside edge, enclosing the

card in the middle. Stab stitch through both thicknesses of felt and card all round the outline of the end of handle which is stuck to the inside. Make three small rolls of felt containing one thickness of pipe-cleaner. Stitch one round the top of the sceptre and two round the other end, just far enough apart to take the Queen's hand. Put the sceptre into her right hand with the end leaning on her shoulder (16) and curl her fingers round the handle. Bend three fingers of her left hand down, leaving the forefinger in a pointing position.

THE RED QUEEN

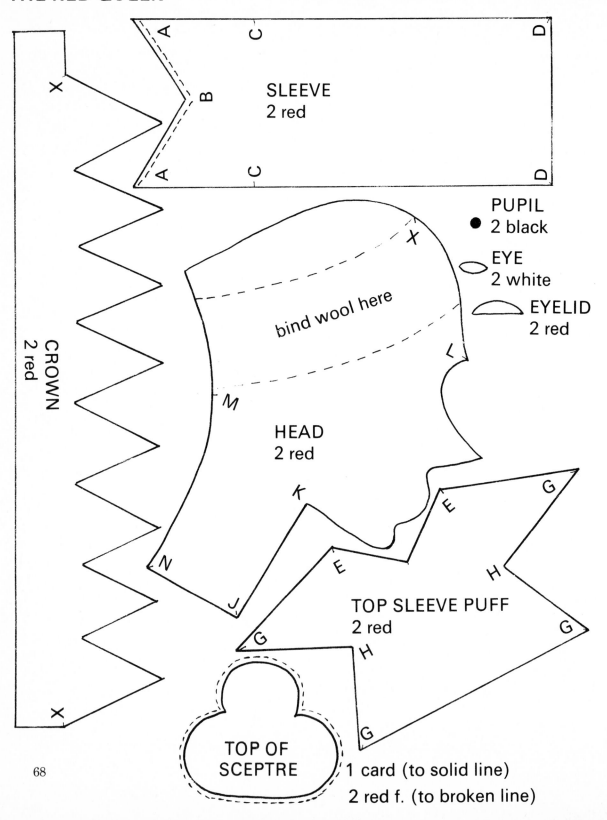

SLEEVE
2 red

A C D

B

A C D

PUPIL
● 2 black

EYE
2 white

EYELID
2 red

CROWN
2 red

X

X

bind wool here

X

L

M

HEAD
2 red

K

N

J

E

G

E

H

G

TOP SLEEVE PUFF
2 red

G

H

G

TOP OF
SCEPTRE

1 card (to solid line)
2 red f. (to broken line)

68

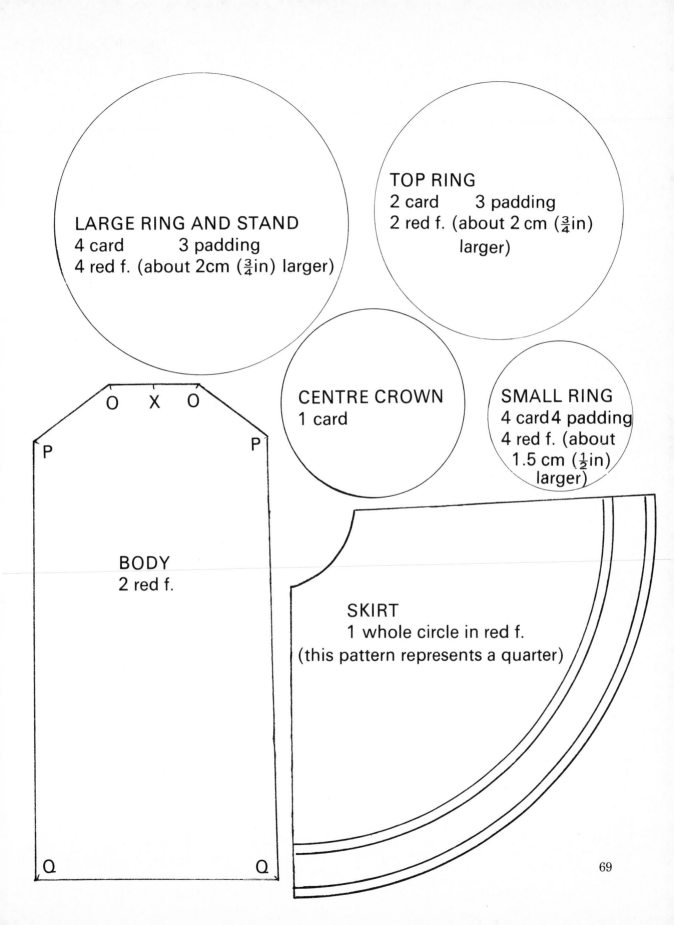

LARGE RING AND STAND
4 card   3 padding
4 red f. (about 2cm ($\frac{3}{4}$in) larger)

TOP RING
2 card   3 padding
2 red f. (about 2 cm ($\frac{3}{4}$in)
          larger)

O   X   O

P   P

CENTRE CROWN
1 card

SMALL RING
4 card 4 padding
4 red f. (about
1.5 cm ($\frac{1}{2}$in)
          larger)

BODY
2 red f.

SKIRT
1 whole circle in red f.
(this pattern represents a quarter)

Q   Q

69

THE WHITE QUEEN

A standing felt toy
Height: 33 cm (13 in)

'. . . she was so dreadfully untidy "Every single thing's crooked," Alice thought to herself, "and she's all over pins!"'

MATERIALS

White felt for all parts:
34 cm × 90 cm (13 in × 36 in)
Black and red embroidery thread for eyes, brows and mouth
A small safety pin
Three or four small, fine hairpins
Wire for stiffening legs: 36 cm (14 in) long
Two small white beads for shoe trimming
A cream carton, approximate capacity
$\frac{1}{4}$ litre ($\frac{1}{2}$ US pint), for skirt foundation
The eleven items marked * given for the Red Queen on page 61 but in white

METHOD

Cut out the pieces as given on page 74 (9 pieces), plus the crown, centre of crown, sleeves, top sleeve puffs and body as given for Red Queen on page 68–69 (9 pieces), the head, fronts, backs and soles of shoes as given for Tweedledum and Tweedledee on page 42 (10 pieces), the hands as given for the Queen of Hearts on page 52 (4 pieces), plus two strips $3\frac{1}{2}$ cm × 10 cm ($1\frac{1}{2}$ in × 4 in) for the elbow puffs and two strips 12 cm × 25 cm ($4\frac{3}{4}$ in × 10 in) for the legs (36 pieces in all), in white felt throughout.

Crown (Fig. 1(12)) Work as given for the Red Queen (pages 61–62) but do not decorate with beads and sequins.

Hands and Arms Work as given for the Red Queen (pages 62–64), but do not decorate the top puffs with braid.

Legs and Feet Work as given for Tweedledum and Tweedledee (pages 38–39). For the White Queen the piece of felt rolled round the legs will make stockings instead of socks and therefore should reach almost to the top of the wires. Do not sew snap-fasteners to the soles or put bows on the shoes, but decorate by sewing a felt flower with a small bead in the centre to the top of each.

Body Working on the wrong side, place the two pieces together and join them O-P-Q on both sides. Gather round neck opening O-X-O-X-O. Pull tightly and fasten off. Turn right side out, stuff firmly. Place on one side leaving the base open.

Sceptre (Fig. 1(3)) Work as given for the Red Queen (page 67) but using the fleur-de-lis shape for the top, with two felt rolls instead of one directly underneath it (4).

Skirt If possible the carton foundation should be 11·5 cm ($4\frac{1}{2}$ in) tall, but with the base cut out – the resulting hole will be 5 cm (2 in) in diameter. As this hole will be the waist, turn the carton upside down. (If

Fig. 1 The White Queen

no carton is available make a similar shape from thin card.) Cover the carton with white felt (5), sticking the material in place with about 2 cm ($\frac{3}{4}$ in) superfluous felt at each end. Turn this to the inside and stick all round the lower edge, but leave it standing upright round the top edge.

Cut a strip of white felt 5·5 cm (2$\frac{1}{4}$ in) wide and long enough to stretch round the base of the carton with a little to spare. Fold the strip in half lengthwise and join the long edges so as to make a tube. If oversewing by hand do it on the right side; if machining, work on the wrong side and turn so as to get rid of the ridge formed by the stitching. Stuff the tube lightly, then join into a ring by ladder stitching all round the open ends. Slip the ring on to the

carton, easing it down to cover the lower edge with the seam to the inside facing the carton and the join on the ring level matching the centre back on the felt covering the carton (6). Secure with either a little adhesive or a stitch here and there. Make three more rings in the same way, each one a little smaller than the next, and fix one above the other round the skirt an equal distance apart.

This Queen's crinoline frame shows below her skirt in her typical slovenly way. To make this, twist doubled pipe-cleaners together so as to make a piece which will eventually be long enough to form a ring slightly larger than the lower edge of skirt. Roll a strip of white felt round this and stitch sides together to make into a felt roll

in same manner as for Red Queen's sceptre (page 67) then twist into a ring, leaving the seam underneath, and invisibly join the ends. Make six felt rolls 4 cm (1½ in) long and position them an equal distance apart round the top edge of the ring. Ladder stitch each one in place so that it stands upright. Smear adhesive round the inside of lower edge of skirt and stitch the six upright pieces of the frame to this (you will need to bend them inwards to fit the skirt) so that about 2 cm (¾ in) of the crinoline shows beneath the lowest ring (7).

Head Join the four pieces along the curved edges A-B, leaving opening on one seam. Turn right side out, stuff fully and close opening (this will be at back of head). In the centre of one section about 2 cm (¾ in) from where the lower points join, raise a little oval chin. Do this by stitching up and down and from side to side, using a long, slim needle and white thread and pulling the stitches tightly (Fig. 2(1)).

from top of chin. Stuff the nose as you sew, pushing small pieces of kapok in with an orange stick. Avoid spreading the nose sideways as it must stand out well (2). Sink the eye sockets by taking stitches backwards and forwards from the back of the head, and pulling them tightly (3). This will also automatically pull in the bridge of nose (the resulting darts and lumps on the back of head will be hidden by the hair).

Make eyes with large, tight French knots worked in thick black embroidery thread. Stick on lids, partially covering eyes (4). Embroider black brows, using one strand of thread (5). Make the rolls of fat round the face by stitching backwards and forwards through the face from seam to seam between chin and nose level and pulling the stitches tightly (6). Make the 'bags' under the eyes by sewing two rows of tight stab stitches to form folds (7). Embroider mouth with two strands of red thread. (Do not worry about the rather strange appearance of the head at this stage.)

Assembling Push a leg well up into each side of body, leaving 11 cm (4½ in) exposed from base of body to sole of foot. Stretch the base of body tightly round the top of each leg and stitch firmly (Fig. 3(1)). Join the front and back of body by oversewing between the legs (2). Attach the arms to the body as given for the Red Queen (page 66) working from * to *.

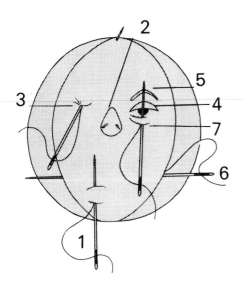

Fig. 2 Modelling the face

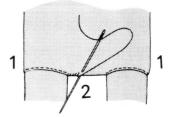

Fig. 3 Attaching the legs

Take the nose piece and on the wrong side join the two brief darts as shown by broken lines on pattern. Turn right side out and sew to head with lower edge 2·5 cm (1 in)

Sew the head to top of body, ladder stitching several times round (Fig. 1(8)). Run a gathering thread round the upper edge of the spare felt at top of skirt, leave thread and needle hanging. Ease the feet and legs down through the top of skirt. Pull up gathers and fasten off so that the top of skirt fits the body tightly all round under the arms. Stitch skirt to body, working several times all round the top.

Hair First make the side curls. Wind the yarn round the end of a pencil, working backwards and forwards along a length of approximately 2·5 cm (1 in) until there are four thicknesses. With a large bodkin and strong white thread backstitch several times along the full length of the curl, making sure the needle slides along between pencil and wool so that all the strands are caught and secured. Slide the curl off the pencil and make five more curls in the same way.

Try the crown on head, having the front edge touching tops of eyebrows. Lightly pencil round the back and sides of head indicating the edge of crown, then remove it. Cut the remaining wool into lengths of approximately 61 cm (24 in). Using Fig. 1 as a guide, smear adhesive over one side of head for about 2·5 cm (1 in) depth from pencil mark downwards. Stick about fifteen strands of wool from front to back across this, thus covering the side of head, with about 5 cm (2 in) hanging forwards over face and the long ends hanging down back. Cover the other side of head in the same way. Stick the remaining pieces of wool to top of head where the ends will be hidden under the crown.

Apply adhesive to the inside of crown and stick this firmly in place. Smear adhesive along the stitched side of each of the curls and stick these to each side of head (9). Leave the Queen until all the adhesive is set and dry. Gather the long hair together at the back of the head and twist it into a large untidy bun. Keep this in place by covering with white netting for a snood, stitching this firmly to the head. Cut the short lengths of wool at front of head to odd and uneven lengths. Stiffen these by

painting with colourless nail polish and arrange them sticking out in an untidy manner. To add a finishing touch to the hair, stick a few hairpins here and there through the bun (10) and (11).

Finishing off Arrange the shawl in position, stitching here and there and pinning in place at the front with a small silver safety pin. Fold the arms in front and curl the right hand round the handle of the sceptre.

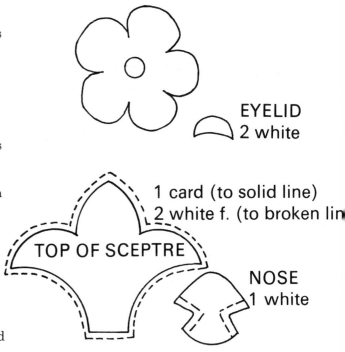

EYELID
2 white

1 card (to solid line)
2 white f. (to broken lin

TOP OF SCEPTRE

NOSE
1 white

74

THIMBLE TOYS

'. . . the pool was getting quite crowded with the birds and animals that had fallen into it: there were a Duck and a Dodo, a Lory and an Eaglet, and several other curious creatures. Alice led the way, and the whole party swam to the shore.'

The small toys which follow are all characters from the Pool of Tears and the Caucus-race. Each one is made over a thimble so that it may be slipped on to the finger and used as a finger puppet. This in itself is appropriate, for Alice's prize after the Caucus-race was a thimble from her own pocket. The thimbles used to make the toys may be old and worn but if you are buying them specially, choose small sizes to fit whoever is to play with the toys. Large sizes can easily be reduced by sticking medical adhesive tape round the inside so that they fit really tightly. A thimble toy is no fun if it is constantly falling off.

ALICE

Height: 9 cm (3½ in) from feet to top of head

'. . . I never was so small as this before, never!'

MATERIALS
Scraps of both pale blue and white cotton poplin or similar fabric for clothes
An old piece of narrow white ribbon or tape for pinafore strings
Scraps of flesh-pink stockinet for head and arms
Black Russia braid for trimming:
62 cm (24½ in)
Scraps of black and white felt for stockings and shoes
Black, blue, white and red stranded embroidery thread for features and shoe straps
Fine yellowish or honey-coloured wool or stranded thread for hair
Two pipe-cleaners
A thimble for base
A knob of kapok for stuffing head
Adhesive

METHOD
Cut out pieces on page 78 (12 pieces).

NOTE: Do allow about 0·5 cm ($\frac{1}{4}$ in) material for turnings on the cotton material for Alice's clothes when cutting out.

Head Run a gathering thread all round the outside edge of head piece as shown by broken line on pattern. Stuff firmly, pull up gathers and fasten off to form a little ball.

Dress Turn back lower hem to broken line on pattern and stick with a scant smear of adhesive. Stick two rows of braid in place as shown on pattern, leaving the ends raw. Join the skirt into a ring by seaming the short ends together on the wrong side. Turn right way out and gather all along top edge, turning the raw edge to the back as you work. Pull up gathers as tightly as possible and fasten off securely.

Preparing the Thimble If possible use an old thimble with at least two holes worn through it at the top. If a new one is used, choose the plastic variety and burn two holes in the top by piercing this with a darning needle made red-hot in a candle flame. (If you push the eye of the needle into a cork you will be able to hold the needle more easily without burning your fingers!)

Joining Head and Dress to Thimble Place the gathers at top of dress on top of thimble, keeping in place with a scant smear of adhesive. Stitch on the head with the gathers at centre back, using strong thread and a long needle and working up and down through the holes in the thimble and of course right through the top of dress at the same time (with seam of this at centre back) (2). Run a gathering thread all round dress at a position about halfway down thimble. This will be the waist. Smear the top half of thimble with adhesive, pull up gathers to fit thimble and fasten off. Press the top of dress on to the thimble, arranging the folds as neatly as possible (3).

Arms Fold the ends of a pipe-cleaner to the centre, thus halving the length but doubling the thickness. Smear a little adhesive along one long edge of the stockinet and lay the pipe-cleaner on it as shown on pattern. When dry, roll the material round the cleaner, first folding in the extra material at each end A-B and C-D (this makes a fat part for the hands), turn in raw edge B-D and neatly oversew. Run a gathering thread round wrists and pull them in a little. Take the sleeve pieces and stick back the hem edge on each to the broken line shown on pattern. Seam short ends E-F together on the wrong side. Turn right way out. Run a gathering thread round each about 0·5 cm ($\frac{1}{4}$ in) from hem edge, put on to arm piece in positions shown (4), pull up gathers to fit so as to form a frilled edge to a puff sleeve, fasten off gathers and stitch to arm. Take an odd piece of matching blue material and folding back the raw edges so that you have a strip about 2 cm ($\frac{3}{4}$ in) wide, wind it round arm piece at centre, covering raw edges of puffed sleeves (5). Tuck in raw edge and stitch. Sew arm piece complete with sleeve to centre back of doll and bend to a U shape.

Pinafore Stick braid to pinafore apron,

76

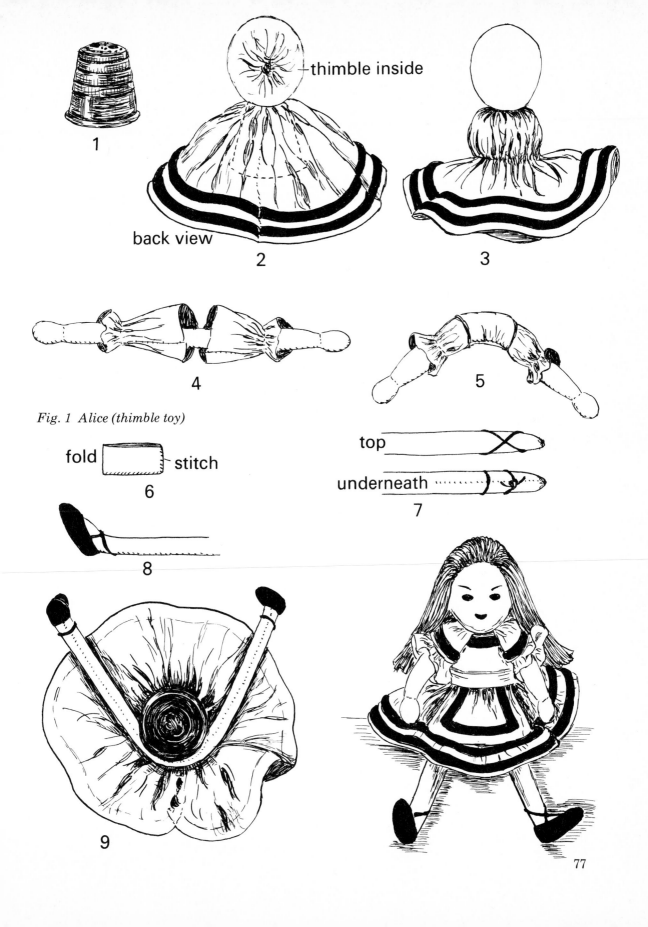

thimble inside

back view

Fig. 1 Alice (thimble toy)

fold stitch

top

underneath

1
2
3
4
5
6
7
8
9

77

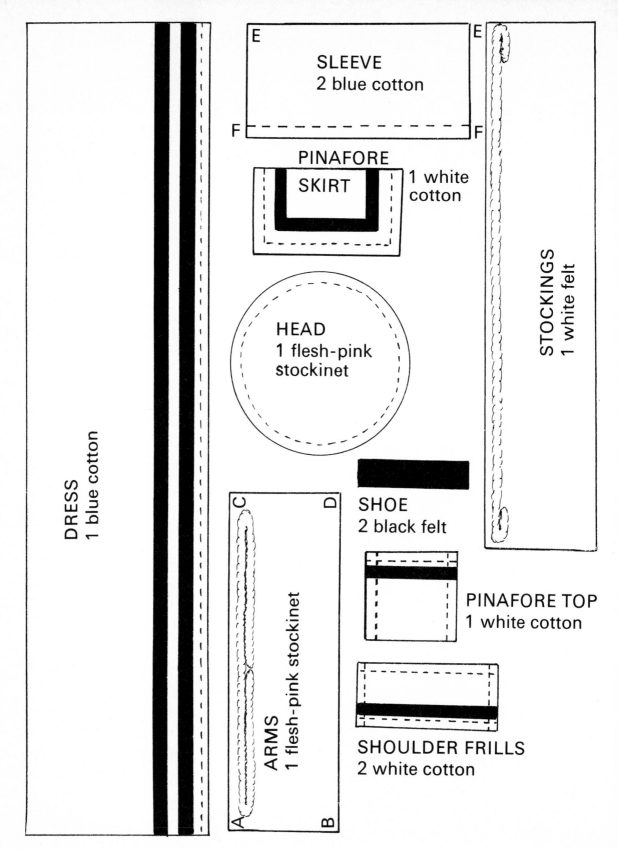

DRESS
1 blue cotton

SLEEVE
2 blue cotton

E — E
F — F

PINAFORE
SKIRT
1 white cotton

HEAD
1 flesh-pink stockinet

STOCKINGS
1 white felt

SHOE
2 black felt

C — D

ARMS
1 flesh-pink stockinet

A — B

PINAFORE TOP
1 white cotton

SHOULDER FRILLS
2 white cotton

bodice and shoulder frills as shown on pattern, then stick back hems to broken lines. Stick bodice to doll. Gather along top of apron piece, turning back a small hem at the same time, and pull up to fit waist. Fasten off and stick to waist of doll, covering the raw edge at base of top piece. Gather along top edge of shoulder frills and stick over doll's shoulders, pulling up the gathers to fit and fastening off. Do not worry about the appearance of back as this will eventually be covered by hair. Tie a piece of narrow tape or ribbon round waist, making a bow at the back and sticking in place at the front.

Legs Smear a little adhesive along one edge of the leg piece, fold a pipe-cleaner and lay it on the adhesive as shown on pattern. Roll the feet tightly round the cleaner and neatly hem all along the edge. Stitch over both ends pulling them in as much as possible.

The shoes are of course black but are shown as white for clarity. Fold each shoe piece in half so that the short ends meet. On the wrong side oversew the short ends together (back of shoe) and along base, running down centre of sole of shoe (6). Turn right way out, very carefully poking out corners with the point of a pencil. Cross pieces of black stranded thread over each foot for shoe straps, tying in a knot under each foot (7). Turn feet forwards just enough to fit shoes. Push a foot into each shoe, pulling and stitching the top edges of shoes together for just under 0·5 cm ($\frac{1}{4}$ in) at toe ends, then stitching shoes to feet all round the edge of each shoe (8). Bend leg piece to a U shape and stick to thimble all round the back half at lower edge (9).

Finishing off Embroider the face as shown in Fig. 1, making blue dots for eyes, red for mouth and brown for brows. Smear adhesive over forehead and all the rest of the head except face. Cut through both ends of a skein of stranded embroidery thread and lay the pieces across the head from front to back so that the face is completely covered. Press thread well on to adhesive, then turn the strands covering face over to the back of head and press this down as well, being careful to get a smooth hairline round the face.

THE MOUSE

Height: 6 cm (2½ in)

'. . . she heard something splashing about in the pool a little way off, . . . at first she thought it must be a walrus or hippopotamus, but then she remembered how small she was now, and she soon made out that it was only a mouse that had slipped in like herself.'

MATERIALS

Scraps of grey and flesh-pink felt for body
A pipe-cleaner
Thin card to stiffen feet
Grey, black and white stranded thread for features
Colourless nail polish
A thimble for base
Kapok for stuffing
Adhesive

METHOD

Cut out the pieces as given on page 82 (18 pieces).

Body On the wrong side join each body piece to the body gusset, stitching A-B on each side. Insert head gusset, stitching A-C on both sides. Join C-D on body. Turn right side out and stuff very firmly indeed, pushing the kapok well up into the nose. Push a thimble smeared with adhesive up into the base of the toy, packing stuffing well round it so that the toy is quite firm and the rim of the thimble is just hidden inside its base.

Features Stick each pink lining to a grey ear. Fold in half at the base, pink side

inside, and stitch to head in position shown on Fig. 2. Cut a tiny circle of pink felt, gather all round the edge, place over nose tip, pull up gathers to fit and stitch in place, being sure to make the nose *really* small and pointed. Embroider eyes using black and white stranded thread, then take a few stitches right through the head from the corner of one eye to the corresponding corner on the other and pull them tightly to sink eyes slightly into the head. Make a few whiskers by taking long looped stitches through head in the position shown, using white thread, then cutting through the loops and trimming the whiskers to size. Secure and stiffen these with a dab of colourless nail polish.

Haunches Hem both pieces very neatly in place, one each side of body so that the E's almost meet at centre back of body and working all round the curved edge E-F-G. Stuff very firmly, pushing tiny pieces of kapok up between the body and haunch pieces with the point of an orange stick. When they are really well padded, stitch base of each haunch E-G to body.

Right *The White Queen*

80

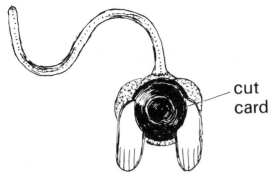

gather

Fig. 2 The Mouse

Arms Stick the arm pieces together in pairs with a hand between each pair, matching the broken line on hand pattern with the end of the arms. Stick an arm to each side of body as shown (Fig. 2).

Feet Stick each felt foot to a piece of thin but strong card. Cut round the card to shape of foot, then snip both thicknesses inwards to make toes. Turn Mouse upside down and hold feet against edge of thimble. Cut away a small piece from the inside of each one so that neither will obstruct the opening of the thimble. Stick feet firmly in place, card side away from body so that the Mouse will stand on the card and the pink felt feet will show at the top.

Tail Cut approximately 8 cm ($3\frac{1}{4}$ in) from a pipe-cleaner, fold a strip of flesh-pink felt tightly round it and oversew very neatly all along the length and over ends. Stitch firmly to back of Mouse.

Finishing off Using one strand of grey thread, take a few stitches here and there over the mouse to simulate hairs, making sure some cover joins between arms and hands, arms and body and body and tail, to soften these hard lines. If the neck seems too fat, pull it in a little with a tightly-pulled gathering thread.

Left (above) *The Thimble Toys*
(below) *Alice (doll)*

81

THE MOUSE

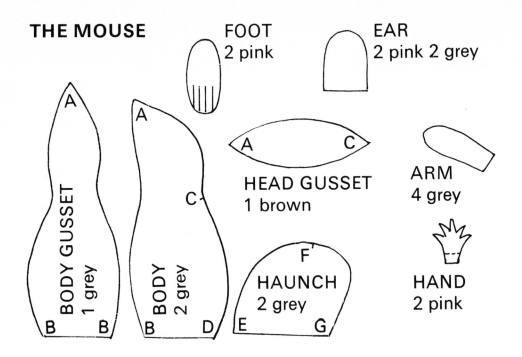

FOOT
2 pink

EAR
2 pink 2 grey

A

A

A   C

C

HEAD GUSSET
1 brown

ARM
4 grey

BODY GUSSET
1 grey

BODY
2 grey

F

HAUNCH
2 grey

HAND
2 pink

B   B

B   D

E   G

THE DUCK

Height: 6·5 cm (2½ in)

'I know what "it" means well enough, when I find a thing', said the Duck, 'it's generally a frog or a worm. . . .'

MATERIALS

Scraps of white felt for body and yellow felt for feet and beak
White stranded thread for feather markings
Black stranded thread for eyes and beak markings
A thimble for base
Kapok for stuffing
Adhesive

This toy is stab stitched on the right side because of the difficulty of turning such a slim neck. The resulting neat little ridge seam is hidden afterwards by the thick feather markings.

METHOD

Cut out the pieces as given on page 84 (14 pieces).

Body *Join the body gusset to both body pieces stitching A-B on each side. Join body pieces together A-C. Insert head gusset, stitching C-D on both sides, then join body pieces D-E-F. The resulting hole B-F-B should be just large enough to fit round the rim of the thimble. Stuff the Duck very firmly, taking particular care over the neck and leaving room at base for the thimble.

Fill the tail out well. Smear this with adhesive and push up into body, so that the rim is just hidden inside base of toy, packing plenty of stuffing round it so that the hole thing is quite firm.* Join the inner wings G-H on the *wrong* side. Place this piece on one of the wing pieces matching letters and, working on the right side again, join them H-I-G, then place the other wing piece on the other end of the joined inner wings and stitch round G-I-H. You now have double wing tips with single wide ends. Stuff the wings, then pin on to Duck's back so that they curve upwards (i.e. H at neck end) pulling the single flaps H-J-G down one each side of body and stitching firmly in place. The Duck will have the appearance of flapping its wings ready for 'take off' (Fig. 3).

Beak and Eyes Join the two beak pieces together all round the long curved edge shown by broken line on pattern. Stuff very firmly and stitch to front of Duck's head. Using three strands of black embroidery thread make a French knot on one side of head for an eye, pass thread through head and make a similar knot on the other side. Pass the thread through head to beak and make two black stitches on the top as shown on pattern for 'breathers'. Pass the

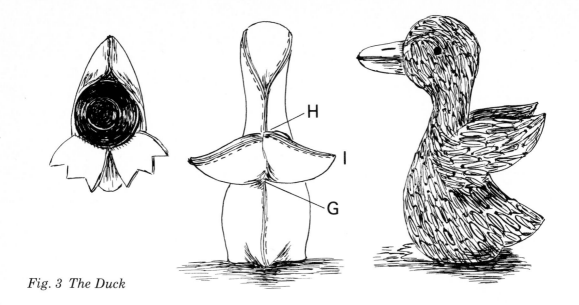

Fig. 3 The Duck

thread back to one of the eye positions and stitch several times backwards and forwards through head from one eye to the other, pulling the stitches tightly to sink eyes a little and then fastening off thread.

Feet Embroider three black lines on two of the foot pieces, then stick each of these pieces to one of the remaining two pieces. Sew these to base of body at front edge of thimble.

Feather Markings Make a series of stitches all over the body and wings using thick white stranded embroidery thread, placing the stitches in the direction the Duck's feathers would grow.

THE DUCK

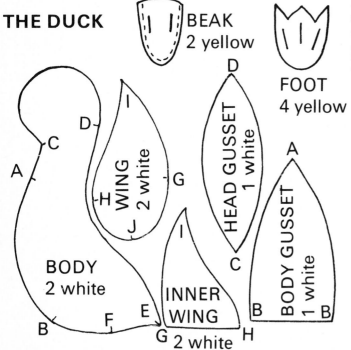

BEAK
2 yellow

FOOT
4 yellow

WING
2 white

HEAD GUSSET
1 white

BODY
2 white

INNER
WING
2 white

BODY GUSSET
1 white

84

THE LORY

Height: 6·5 cm (2½ in)

... the Lory ... at last turned sulky and would only say "I am older than you, and must know better."'

MATERIALS

Scraps of red felt for body, navy blue for head markings, green for wings and yellow for beak
A pipe-cleaner for feet
Yellow, black, red and two shades of green stranded thread for feather
A thimble for base
Kapok for stuffing
Adhesive

METHOD

Cut out the pieces as given on page 86 (13 pieces), plus the body gusset as given for the Duck on page 84 using red felt (14 pieces altogether).

The Body Work exactly as given for the Duck from * to * on page 83 but this time sewing the body on the wrong side and turning it before inserting thimble.

Tail Join the two tail pieces together all round on the right side F-G-H. Stuff, then pin in place over tail end of bird, pulling well on and having ends G at top and bottom. Stitch in place. Take a line of tightly pulled stitches right through the tail as marked by broken line on pattern. Using three strands of embroidery thread sew a

series of stitches all over the Lory to soften the outline and simulate feathers, black on the head and the tip of the tail, both spilling over on to and mixing with the red stitches that cover the rest of the tail and body. Take a few fine yellow stitches on the breast using just two strands of thread.

Beak On the right side stitch the two upper and the two lower beak pieces together in pairs, leaving the short, straight ends of each pair open. Stuff firmly, pushing tiny pieces of kapok inside with an orange stick. Looking at Fig. 4 stitch both beak pieces in place, working all round the open ends.

Eyes Cut a tiny circle of black and yellow felt for each eye and stick as in Fig. 4, then embroider a small black dot in the centre of each.

Wings Place the wings together in pairs, joining them together on the right side except for the short opening section shown by broken line on pattern. Stuff lightly and sew up the opening. On the right side of each wing (be sure to reverse one so as to make a pair) make black feather markings on the tip, two shades of green on the main part and yellow along the top, curved edge, working with stranded thread just as you did for the body. Sew the wings in place, looking at picture for position, then make a few extra yellow stitches from body on to wing to hide the join and soften the outline.

Feet Bend a piece of pipe-cleaner to the shape and size shown on Fig. 4(1) pinching the ends tightly together (2). Sew to front of Lory to look like perching claws. Paint with black ink.

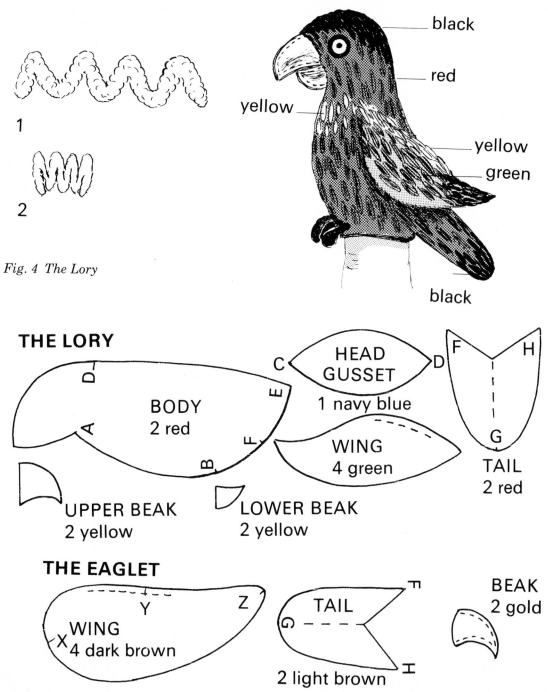

Fig. 4 The Lory

THE LORY

BODY
2 red

HEAD GUSSET
1 navy blue

WING
4 green

TAIL
2 red

UPPER BEAK
2 yellow

LOWER BEAK
2 yellow

THE EAGLET

WING
4 dark brown

TAIL
2 light brown

BEAK
2 gold

THE MAGPIE

Height: 11 cm (4½ in) from tip of beak to end of tail

'. . . one old Magpie began wrapping itself up very carefully, remarking, "I really must be getting home; the night-air doesn't suit my throat!"'

MATERIALS
Scraps of black and white felt for body,
grey felt for beak and yellow felt for eyes
Black and white stranded thread for feather markings
A pipe-cleaner and grey stranded thread for feet
A thimble for base
Kapok for stuffing
Adhesive

METHOD
Cut out the pieces as given on page 88 (8 pieces) and the body and head gusset as given for the Lory on page 86 but using black felt (3 pieces) and the body gusset as given for the Duck on page 84 (12 pieces altogether).

Body Work exactly as given for the Duck from * to * on page 83 but sewing the body the wrong side and turning before inserting thimble.

Tail Work exactly as given for the Lory on page 85 noting the upright angle at which it is attached on Fig. 5 and covering the body and tail with black feather markings and the breast with white (7).

Beak On the right side join the two beak pieces all round the long, curved edge shown by broken line on pattern, stuff firmly and sew to body at C on pattern, working all round open end.

Eyes Cut a tiny circle of yellow felt and stick to each side of head then embroider a very small black dot (just one tiny stitch) in the centre of each.

Wings Work as for the Lory on page 85 but make white feature markings along the top straight edge of each wing and black on the rest. Soften the join to body with white stitches.

Feet and Legs Cut six pieces of pipe-cleaner 5 cm (2 in) long – three for each leg. Take one of these pieces and smear adhesive generously over half of it (Fig. 5). (Be sure to use rubber-based adhesive which rubs easily off the skin, as your finger will become covered with adhesive during this process.) Starting at the centre, bind grey stranded thread down to the end, then back again, thus covering half of it (2). The adhesive will ooze through between the strands. Cut off thread and press starting and finishing ends into the adhesive, then roll the covered piece of cleaner between

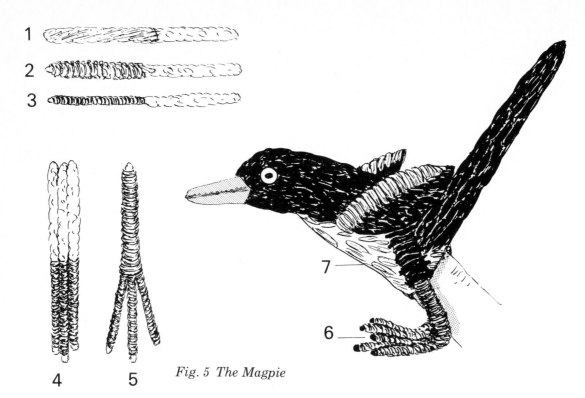

Fig. 5 The Magpie

your finger and thumb, thus smoothing and pressing the adhesive all over the claw you are making (3). Place on one side to dry. Bind one end of the other five pieces in the same way. When these pieces are quite dry, place them side by side in threes (the bound ends are the Magpie's claws), having the centre claw a little more forward than the others (4). Smear the unbound ends with adhesive and bind them together for the legs, using grey stranded thread and working from the top downwards and back again, pressing the thread into the adhesive as you did before (5). (The centre claw should be about 2 cm ($\frac{3}{4}$ in) long.) Bend each leg at right angles to the claws and place on one side to dry thoroughly, then touch the end of each claw with black ink, thus covering any white pipe-cleaner which may be showing (6).*

With a little adhesive stick one leg to each side of the bird with the ends well up under wings. Then cover the tops of the legs with stitches taken right over them, using thick black stranded thread.

Adjust the Magpie by bending the feet and legs until he stands really firmly.

THE MAGPIE

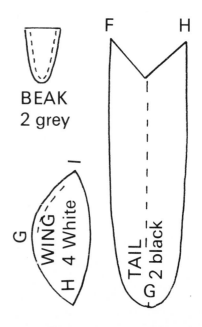

BEAK
2 grey

WING
H 4 White
G I

TAIL
G 2 black
F H

THE EAGLET

Height: 6·5 cm (2½ in)

'Speak English' said the Eaglet. 'I don't know the meaning of half those long words, and, what's more, I don't believe you do either!'

MATERIALS
Scraps of dark and light brown felt for body and yellow felt for beak
Dark brown, fawn and gold stranded thread for feather markings
Two pipe-cleaners and yellow stranded thread for feet
A thimble for base
Kapok for stuffing
Adhesive

METHOD

Cut out the pieces as given on page 86 (8 pieces), the body as for the Lory on page 86 using dark brown felt and the head gusset as for Lory in rust felt (3 pieces) and the body gusset as given for the Duck on page 84 using light brown felt (12 pieces altogether).

The Body Work as given for the Duck on page 83 from * to *.

The Tail Work as given for the Lory on page 85 making the feather markings in gold on the head, fawn where tail joins body and dark brown over the rest of the body.

Beak On the right side sew the two pieces together all round the two curved edges indicated by broken line on pattern. Stuff firmly and sew to head looking at Fig. 6 for position and working all round the open end.

Eyes Cut two small yellow and two black ovals taking the size and shape from Fig. 6. Stick each black piece on top of a yellow then stick the completed eye to the bird. Take a tiny white stitch at the top of each eye for a highlight.

Wings Make these exactly as given for the Lory's wings on page 85 but make the feather markings in brown and fawn with a few gold stitches at tops and tips. Soften the join to body with brown stitches. The wings of this bird should be attached firmly to the body all round the front curved edge X-Y, the two tips at Z being stitched to side of tail so that the finished wings appear to be neatly folded.

Feet Cut six pieces of pipe-cleaner each 2·5 cm (1 in) long then make up two feet exactly as given for the Magpie (Fig. 5(1–6)) but make each claw 1 cm (just under ½ in) long. When finished, bend the claws to

Fig. 6 The Eaglet

a typical eagle shape, and when dry wrap
the leg part in a small piece of dark brown
felt. Stitch this in place, making a seam at
the back, then stitch the legs to front of
bird. A few stitches to represent feathers
taken over the join between tops of legs and
body will improve the appearance.

THE DODO

Height 8 cm (just over 3 in)

'What I was going to say,' said the Dodo in an offended tone, 'was, that the best thing to get us dry would be a Caucus-race.'

MATERIALS

Scraps of grey and brown felt for the body, white for wings and tail, yellow for beak
Black, brown and grey stranded thread for feather markings
Three pipe-cleaners and yellow stranded thread for feet
A thimble for base
Kapok for stuffing
Adhesive

METHOD

Cut out the pieces as given on page 93 (14 pieces).

Body Sew the first part on the *wrong* side so as to get a nice, smooth line on top of bird. Join body sides to head gusset A-B on both sides, then join the two body pieces together along top of neck and body B-C. Turn the work *right* way out and stuff the neck firmly then join the two body pieces together A-D, putting a small piece of pipe-cleaner into the neck to strengthen it (see Fig. 7) and pushing in small pieces of kapok with the point of an orange stick as you work. Now join the body gusset to both sides of body E-F, pushing a little stuffing into the body before completing the second side. You now have a hole F-C-F which should just fit the rim of a thimble tightly.

Finish stuffing the body through this hole, leaving room for the thimble, then smear this with adhesive and push it well into the body, packing stuffing all round it so that the whole thing is quite firm and the rim is just hidden inside.

Tail On the right side join the two pieces together all round except for the short, straight end shown by broken line on pattern. Stuff firmly and sew to body just above the thimble, working all round the open end.

Beak Embroider a black line on both pieces as shown on pattern, remembering to reverse one so as to make a pair. Place the two pieces together and join on the right side, stitching all round except for the two straight sides shown by broken line on pattern. Stuff firmly and pull well on to head, pinning in position shown. Stitch firmly in place. Join the two small tip pieces together on the right side, working all round except for the short end shown by broken line on pattern. Pin, then stitch on to end of beak in position shown. Look at Fig. 7 and using three strands of black thread embroider black lines between beak and beak tip. Stick a tiny white circle each side for eyes and embroider a black dot in the centre of each and a brow on the top.

Feather markings Using three strands of brown cotton sew a series of small stitches over body and tail to look like feather markings, concentrating these on the top of the head (which has the appearance of a little brown cap) and in a line down centre of back. Look at Fig. 7 while working so as not to waste time covering the place where the wings will eventually be stitched or the position of the places where the legs will be pushed into body. Make the stitches on the tail in the shape of a plume. Finally, take a few stitches here and there in a lighter shade of grey than the body felt, except on the concentrated brown parts, to give a lifelike appearance to the creature.

Feet and Legs Cut eight pieces of pipe-cleaner 3 cm (just over 1 in) long and make the feet and legs exactly as given for the Magpie (Fig. 5(1–6), working as far as * and making the claws 1 cm ($\frac{1}{2}$ in) long when finished, but with four on each leg instead of three and bound in yellow cotton instead of grey. When dry, using pointed scissors make two holes one on each seam

Fig. 7 The Dodo

line just in front of thimble, smear adhesive on top of each leg and push one up into each hole leaving about 1 cm ($\frac{1}{2}$ in) of leg showing. Using a slim needle, as it is quite difficult to sew through the leg, take a series of stitches in three strands of brown thread and a few in white from the leg up on to body, working all round the top of each leg to give a feathered effect.

Wings Place the pieces together in pairs and on the right side join all round outside edge except for a small section, stuff firmly and close opening. Take a series of stitches on one side of each wing to represent feathers, some black and some grey. Stitch a wing to each side of body, then sew a few grey stitches over top of wing on to body to soften the outline. Then embroider a few more feather-like stitches anywhere on bird that you think they are needed.

THE DODO

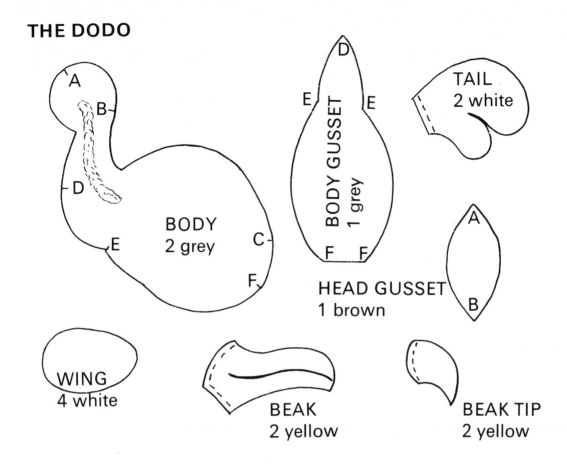

A
B
D
E

BODY
2 grey

C
F

D
E
BODY GUSSET
1 grey
E
F
F

TAIL
2 white

A
B
HEAD GUSSET
1 brown

WING
4 white

BEAK
2 yellow

BEAK TIP
2 yellow

ALICE

A rag doll
Height: 33 cm (13 in)

'. . . so many out-of-the-way things had happened lately, that Alice had begun to think that very few things indeed were really impossible.'

MATERIALS

Flesh-pink cotton or stockinet for body:
51 cm × 66 cm (20 in × 26 in)
Fine yellowish or honey-coloured wool for hair
Small piece of black leather or felt for shoes
Card for shoe stiffeners
White cotton or polyester material for panties, petticoat, dress collar and pinafore:
30 cm × 90 cm (12 in × 36 in)
Pale blue cotton or polyester material for dress:
30 cm × 90 cm (12 in × 36 in)
Small piece of blue and white striped stockinet for socks (if this is not available plain white material may be used and the blue stripes painted on with fabric paints)
Narrow elastic for panties
Black Russia braid for trimming:
1·85 Metres (2 yards)
Narrow lace for petticoat and panties: about 1·4 metres (1½ yards)
Blue, dark brown, white and red embroidery thread for features
Light blue embroidery thread to match dress material
Strong black button thread for shoe laces
Four tiny buttons or snap-fasteners for petticoat and dress
Thin piece of wood: 6·5 cm (2½ in) long
Strip of rag for binding: 2·5 cm (1 in) wide

METHOD

Cut out the pieces for the body as given on pages 98–99 (20 pieces) and the pieces for the clothes (page 102) together with a strip of white cotton 9 cm × 15 cm (3½ in × 6 in) for pinafore skirt and a piece the same size in blue cotton for the dress (32 pieces). You should now have 52 pieces in all.

NOTE: Allow 0·5 cm (¼ in) turnings when cutting out cotton body and clothes.

Head On wrong side of material stitch all V-shaped darts around edge of face. Sew the two back of head pieces together A-E. Next join front and back of head both sides A-B, then placing centre of neck C to centre of the face C, join B-C-B. Finally stitch side seams of neck B-D. Turn the head right way out and stuff very firmly, pushing out the chin and cheeks. Raise the nose following the outline in Fig. 1. Take stitches at the corners of the eyes to sink them. Now embroider the whites of the eyes, blue eyes and brown lashes, brows and pupils, red nostrils and rosy lips, using Fig. 1 as a guide.

Hair Tack stitches around the face to mark the hair line (Fig. 2(1)). Cut wool in lengths

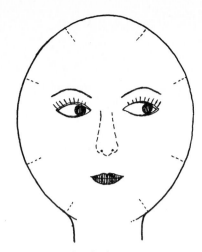

Fig. 1 Sewing Alice's features

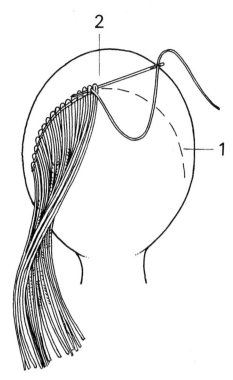

of approximately 36 cm (14 in). Double this, lay the loops to the tacking line and backstitch them very firmly all round the face as shown (2). Sew another line of loops on top of the head, about 0·5 cm ($\frac{1}{4}$ in) directly behind the first line to increase thickness. Smooth all the hair towards the back so that it hangs down behind and place a piece of black braid around Alice's head as a hair band.

Fig. 2 Attaching the hair

Body On wrong side stitch darts either side of bottom on back piece of body only. Place front and back together and stitch all round the body from X-X, leaving neck edge open. Turn right way out and stuff firmly. Bind the piece of wood with rag and push one end up onto the head and the other into the neck and top part of the body. Stuff firmly all round the neck. Turn in the neck edge of the body and sew to the head.

Legs and Feet Again working on the wrong side stitch the foot pieces to the bottom of the legs, matching C-D, and the front foot pieces to front leg, with letters E-F corresponding. Attach the soles of the feet matching letters G and stitch round edge. Now sew up the side seams of the legs, turn to the right side, insert a piece of cardboard cut to the shape of sole into each foot to stiffen and stuff the feet and legs. Turn in top edge and oversew, then stitch along top as shown by the broken line on pattern, to allow leg to move more freely, and take a few tight stitches through the knee to enable limb to bend. Finally sew both legs to the body, feet pointing forwards.

Arms and Hands Stitch the seams of the arms and hands on the wrong side, leaving top edge open, turn and stuff, pushing the filling below the underarm (see broken lines). Oversew top edges together, stitch along broken line at top of arm then take stitches at the elbow position, as for the knee, to allow the arm to bend. Sew arms to shoulders.

Panties (Note: All clothes to be sewn on wrong side then turned, unless you wish to use French seams for extra neatness.) Sew two front pieces together at centre seam, C-A, and two back pieces at centre seams D-A. Now stitch inside leg seams between front and back on both sides A-B. Sew side seams on outer legs, turn in the top of the panties at the broken line shown on the pattern, hem and thread with elastic to fit the doll's body. Finish the bottom of the legs with a narrow hem and edge with lace. Finally stem stitch in a line around each leg about 0·5 cm ($\frac{1}{4}$ in) from hem, pulling the material in slightly to fit Alice's legs.

Petticoat Join the shoulders and side seams of the bodice A-B and C-D on both sides. Seam the short edges of the skirt piece together to make a ring. Now divide the skirt into four, and match the skirt seam to one of the side seams of the bodice. A quarter of the way round from this seam cut an opening for back about 5 cm (2 in) long and sew a very small hem along both sides of this with a tiny pleat at the lower end. Gather the top of the skirt to fit the bodice and join to the bodice with a line of stitching as indicated by the broken line on the pattern (add a second line of stitching for added strength if you wish). Turn in edges of bodice opening at centre back and attach two snap-fasteners or buttons with buttonholes for fastening. Cut bias strips of the white material about 1·5 cm ($\frac{1}{2}$ in) wide and long enough to go round each of the armholes and the neck. For the armholes attach the strips to the raw edges, right sides together, turn in and hem flat on the inside of the bodice. Sew a strip in the same way to the neck edge, but turn only half the width to the back so that hem is on the inside, but the bias strip appears as piping. Turn up the hem of the skirt and finish with a lace edging.

Dress Stitch shoulder seams of bodice to join back and front. Gather the top of each sleeve along the broken lines shown on the pattern and sew into the armhole matching letters C and D on back and front and keeping the gathers mostly over the top of the shoulder seam. Now join the sleeve and sides of bodice E-C/D-F. Make a very

Right *The Mad Hatter and the March Hare*

96

narrow hem around the bottom of sleeve, then gather a line of stitching 1·5 cm ($\frac{1}{2}$ in) from hem to fit the doll's arm above the elbow. Stem stitch over the gathers in blue embroidery thread. Join the short ends of the skirt piece together but leaving an opening approximately 6·5 cm (2$\frac{1}{2}$ cm) long. Hem this opening as for the petticoat bodice. Now gather the skirt to fit bodice and attach with two lines of stitching (the edges of back opening should match the broken lines indicated on back bodice). Turn back hems of centre back opening, and add two buttons or snap-fasteners. Turn up 4 cm (1$\frac{1}{2}$ in) for hem of skirt, then stitch on three rows of black braid for decoration, with the first row 1·5 cm ($\frac{1}{2}$ in) from the bottom of the dress. Sew the four collar pieces together in pairs, turn right way out, top stitch along seamed outer edges, then place both to the *right* side of neck of dress, points X meeting in the centre front, and tack in position. Now cut a bias strip of white material (as for petticoat neck) and lay this on top of collar. Backstitch firmly in a line along neck edge to join all four layers of material, remove tacking and turn bias strip to inside of dress, folding under raw edge and hemming neatly at the back.

Pinafore Hem a strip of white material 2 cm ($\frac{3}{4}$ in) wide and about 30 cm (12 in) long to make a gathered frill to fit sides and bottom of pinafore skirt. Hem these skirt edges, then attach the frill. Gather the top of the pinafore skirt so that it corresponds to the width of the lower edge of pinafore top, then attach it to the top. Cut two strips 3 cm (1$\frac{1}{4}$ in) wide and 31 cm (12 in) long and hem neatly around the edges. Taking two of the four back pieces sew one to each side of one of the pinafore tops only at shoulder seams A-B. Repeat with the second pinafore top and remaining two back pieces. Cut two strips

3 cm (1$\frac{1}{4}$ in) wide and 15 cm (6 in) long. Hem one edge of each, gather the other edge and place to the sides of one top to make shoulder frill, matching points Z on pattern. Now place two parts of pinafore top right sides facing, clip neck edges for turning and stitch them together round the neck. Next, hem the inside piece (without frill attached) to the other at the armholes, making sure that the shoulder frill is neatly tucked inside. Insert waist ties before stitching down remaining sides of top. Make buttonhole loops as indicated on the pattern to enable the ties to be pushed through to the back of the pinafore. Finally hem the edges of the pocket pieces and sew these on to the front of the pinafore skirt.

Socks Stitch the darts and back seams, turn right way out, and make a narrow hem at the top.

Shoes Sew up back seams F-G. Gather between the broken line on each upper, cut along line X-Y on both sides to form straps and sew to sole matching letters E and G. Make a small hole at the end of each strap and tie with black button thread.

Finishing off Iron out any creases in the panties, petticoat, pinafore and dress, paying particular attention to the collar. Now dress Alice in her clothes.

Left *The White Rabbit as a Herald*

ALICE (doll)

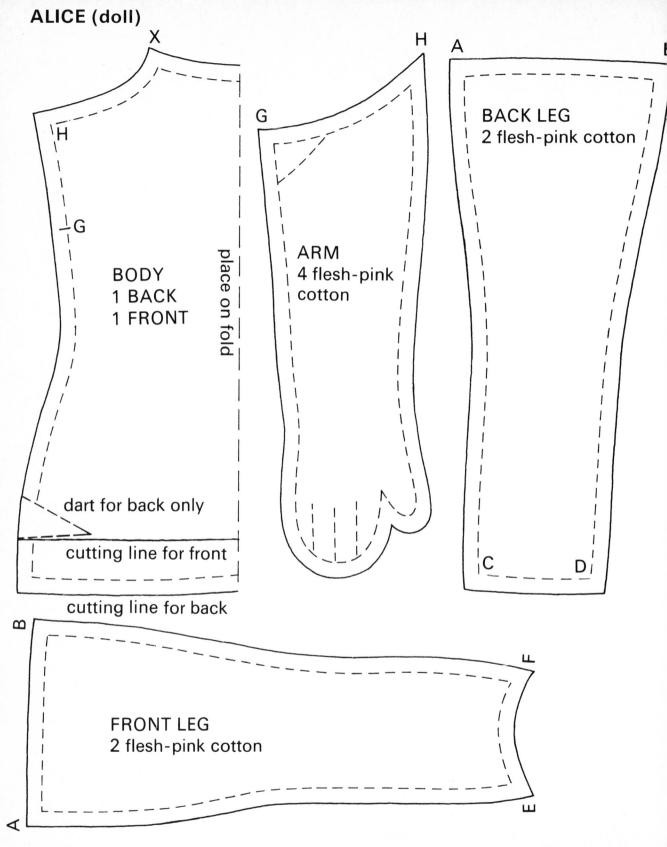

X

H

G

BODY
1 BACK
1 FRONT

place on fold

dart for back only

cutting line for front

cutting line for back

H

G

ARM
4 flesh-pink cotton

A

BACK LEG
2 flesh-pink cotton

C   D

B

FRONT LEG
2 flesh-pink cotton

F

E

A

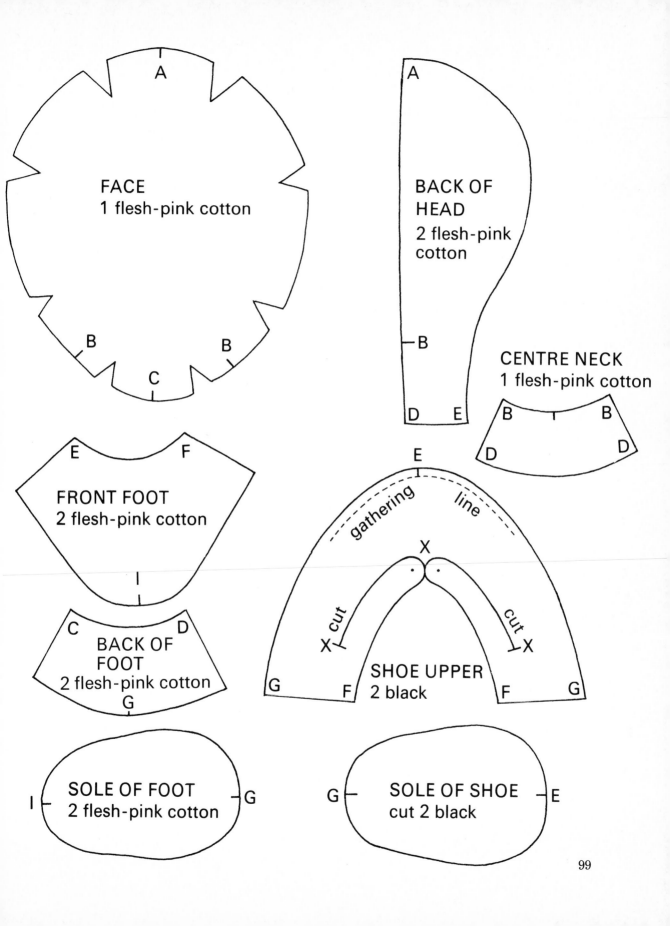

FACE
1 flesh-pink cotton

A

B   B
C

BACK OF
HEAD
2 flesh-pink
cotton

A

B

D   E

CENTRE NECK
1 flesh-pink cotton

B   B

D   D

FRONT FOOT
2 flesh-pink cotton

E   F

C   D

BACK OF
FOOT
2 flesh-pink cotton
G

gathering   line

E

X

X cut   cut X

G   F   F   G

SHOE UPPER
2 black

SOLE OF FOOT
2 flesh-pink cotton

I   G

SOLE OF SHOE
cut 2 black

G   E

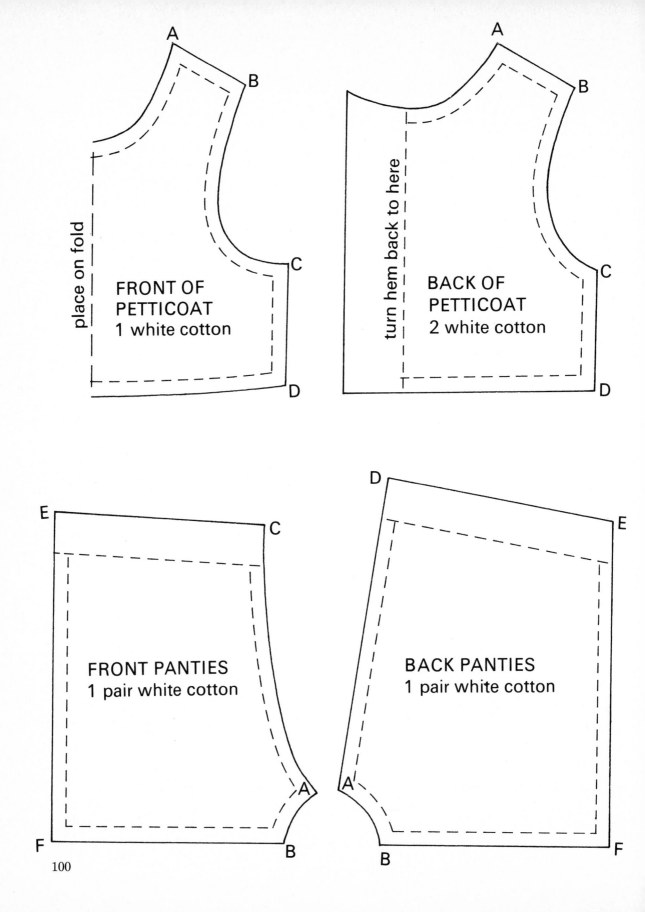

A

B

place on fold

**FRONT OF
PETTICOAT**
1 white cotton

C

D

A

B

turn hem back to here

**BACK OF
PETTICOAT**
2 white cotton

C

D

E

C

FRONT PANTIES
1 pair white cotton

A

F

B

D

E

BACK PANTIES
1 pair white cotton

A

B

F

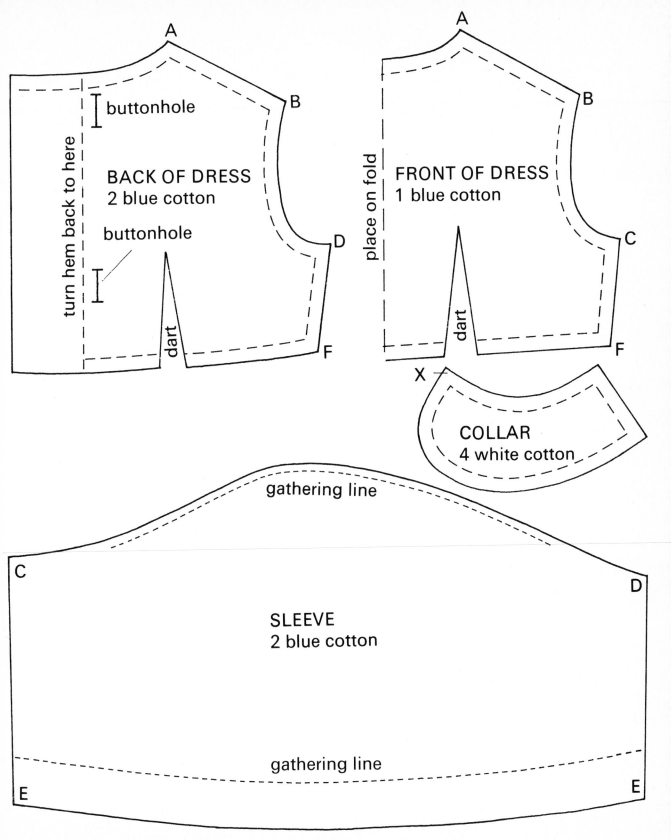

A

B

buttonhole

turn hem back to here

BACK OF DRESS
2 blue cotton

buttonhole

D

dart

F

A

B

place on fold

FRONT OF DRESS
1 blue cotton

C

dart

F

X

COLLAR
4 white cotton

gathering line

C

D

SLEEVE
2 blue cotton

gathering line

E

E

101

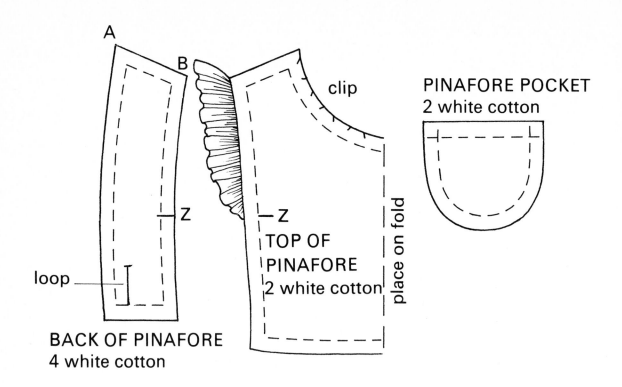

A

B

clip

PINAFORE POCKET
2 white cotton

Z

Z

place on fold

loop

TOP OF
PINAFORE
2 white cotton

BACK OF PINAFORE
4 white cotton

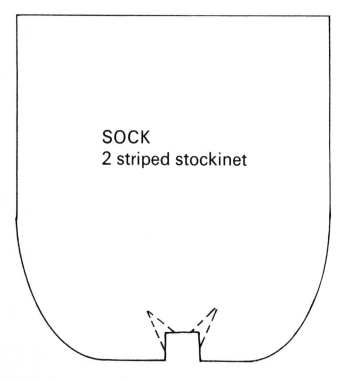

SOCK
2 striped stockinet

ALICE WITH A TELESCOPIC NECK

Height: 21 cm (8 in) and with neck extended
25 cm (10 in)

'Curiouser and curiouser!' cried Alice
... 'Now I'm opening out like the largest
telescope that ever was!'

This small toy is simply made by sticking
material on to a cardboard foundation.
There is almost no sewing. When the
handle is pushed Alice's neck extends as it
did after she had eaten the cake she found
in a glass box. It is the type of toy found in
many Victorian nurseries that Alice herself
might well have played with.

MATERIALS
Stiff cardboard (such as an old box lid) for
base
Approximately eighteen lolly sticks
(US tongue depressor) for manipulation
Scraps of thin flesh-pink card or paper for
face and arms
Scraps of shiny black paper or card for
shoes
Scraps of white felt for stockings
Scraps of pale blue poplin, lawn or similar
fabric for dress
Scraps of similar white material for
pinafore
Black embroidery cotton or fine wool for
shoe straps
Narrow white tape or ribbon for pinafore
strings: 30·5 cm (12 in)
Black Russia braid for trimming:
1 metre (1 yard approximately)
Scraps of frilly white lace for pantalets
Yellowish or honey-coloured fine wool (or
knitting cotton) for hair

Strong clear glue for sticking wooden parts
Adhesive

Optional A little white high-gloss paint

METHOD

Cut out the pieces given on pages 109–10
(23 pieces) noting that the cardboard bases
should be really strong and that if you can
arrange for a selvage to run along the edge
of the skirt, sleeves, pinafore and shoulder
frill you need only cut broken lines.
Otherwise, remember to allow turnings of
about 0·5 cm ($\frac{1}{4}$ in) on cotton fabrics for
clothes before cutting out.

Preparing lolly sticks Using suitable
strong glue stick five lolly sticks (tongue
depressors) together so that they overlap

each other. Then with an old pair of scissors cut pieces from another stick to fit on to each end, smoothing the ends with sandpaper or an old nail file or emery board. Glue these in place so that you have one long stick of double thickness (Fig. 1). Stick a strip of pink paper to one side of the top 10 cm (4 in) for the neck (1). Stick the pink paper face to its cardboard foundation, thus making the head, and stick this to top of neck having the stick extending halfway up back of head (2).

Cut and smooth two pieces of lolly stick about 3 cm (1¼ in) long. Hold the cardboard body bases against the prepared neck so that the top of dress (G on pattern) just covers the place where the pink paper neck ends (3) and mark the position of lower edge of feet on the lolly sticks (5). Glue the two

short pieces of stick just prepared to the sides of the long stick as a crossbar (5), having their upper edge level with the pencil mark. These will later act as a brake, preventing the neck from being pushed completely out of the toy. Now glue nine lolly sticks together in three piles of three. One pile is for a handle (Fig. 2(1)) and the other two for guides inside toy (Fig. 3(2)). Cut six odd pieces of stick about 3 cm (1¼ in) long and glue them together in two piles of three – these will later be strengtheners (Fig. 3(3)). Put all the prepared sticks on one side except the long piece holding the head and the handle. If you wish to paint these white or some attractive colour to tone with your toy do so now and leave to dry thoroughly. However, you can equally well leave them

with their natural wood finish. Leave the head and neck pink of course.

(It is now assumed that the clothes you have cut out all have raw edges and therefore need to be hemmed.)

Skirt (both pieces alike) Turn back hem to broken line at base and stick with a scant smear of adhesive. Stick three rows of black Russia braid along base as shown (leaving raw ends at sides). Turn top edge back and gather along broken line at extreme top of skirt, pull up gathers to fit waist of doll (OOOOOO on pattern) with about 1 cm ($\frac{1}{2}$ in) to spare at each side. Fasten off gathers.

Sleeves (all four alike) Stick back lower edge to broken line. Gather along line XXXX on pattern. Pull up gathers to fit round this line with about 1 cm ($\frac{1}{2}$ in) to spare on each side. Fasten off gathers.

Pinafore Stick back, sides and lower edge to broken lines. Stick a piece of black Russia braid round these three sides as shown on patterns leaving the ends at top raw. Turn back top along 0000 and gather close to edge. Pull up gathers to fit waist of doll. Fasten off gathers. Make both the shoulder frills in the same way. Turn back lower edge to broken line and stick in place. Stick a piece of braid across where shown on pattern, leaving the ends raw.

Dressing Front of Doll On one of the body bases cut off the legs completely, continuing the skirt edge evenly from B round to C. The remaining top part is for the *back* of the toy which has no legs. Stick the legs you have just cut off to the *back* of the legs on the other body foundation. This is for the *front* of the toy which by being double will have extra reinforcement. Take this piece and dress the front of the toy first.

First stick a pair of white felt stockings to each side of the legs. Cross a piece of

black stranded cotton over each foot for shoe straps, tying firmly at the back (Fig. 3(4)). Cut off ends. Stick black paper shoe fronts to front of each foot and the backs to the back, thus covering knots. Stick a piece of frilly lace over top of stockings so that it will eventually show a little below the skirt and look like the edge of a pair of pantalets (Fig. 2(2)). Add the sleeves, smearing a little adhesive along line XXXX on pattern and attaching the row of gathers there, leaving the lower frill loose. Turn back the inner edge of each and stick to base along E-D, then fold the other edges to back of card, arranging them in soft pleats so that the sleeves are puffed. Stick a piece of white material in place for top of pinafore, turning the edges over to the back of card between E-G-E and D and OOOO on pattern and tucking them *under* on top of card between E and D. Leave the lower edge raw and extending a little lower than OOOO at waist. Using Fig. 2 as a guide, stick a piece of black braid round neck leaving the edges raw. Now attach shoulder frills, turning back one raw side edge of each and attaching it to front of doll between E and D on pattern, leaving the lower edge loose then turning the other edges to back of the figure and arranging them in folds so that the frills stand up well. The sleeves should just show underneath. To cover the raw edge of pinafore bodice stick skirt to waist line at OOOO. Tuck in the edges of the material at the armholes on top of the card, trim the sides of the bodice to the reverse of figure and stick, but leave lower edge free. Stick pinafore in place at waist, leaving sides and lower edge free. Take one pair of arms and stick in place, tucking the ends well up under sleeve frill.

Cut a small piece of card for neck edge of dress, cover this with blue material and stick to back of card (Fig. 3(1)) so that it just shows on front of doll. If lower edge of skirt seems to stand out too much, stick here and there to card base along hem line.

Fig. 1 Making the base for Alice with a
Telescopic Neck

Fig. 2 Front view

Fig. 3 Inside back

Fig. 4 Back view

107

Dressing Back of Doll Attach the sleeves as for the front. Cover the top with blue material for the bodice of the dress instead of white for the pinafore top, as on the front. Attach skirt as for front. Stick on arm pieces only as far as skirt sides, cutting off and discarding the superfluous centre piece, as on the finished doll the hands will appear folded behind the back.

Making Hair and Face Spread adhesive over top of front of head (above broken line on pattern) and lay bundles of fine wool about 14 cm (5½ in) long on to this, pressing firmly in place – the hair will now cover the face. Stick similar bundles of wool to the back of head, then smear a little adhesive on to the upper part of back hair and turn the front hair smoothly and evenly over to the back of head, pressing it down lightly. You can make the hair as thin or as thick as you wish. (Look at Fig. 2.) Stick ovals of white paper carefully in place for eyes, then draw pupils, lashes and brows with black ink, nostrils and mouth with red.

Assembling Toy Lay the prepared front face downwards (Fig. 3) and glue the two prepared piles of lolly sticks in place as guides (2). Stick the prepared strengtheners to arms (3). Now lay the long stick attached to the head face downwards in the channel formed by the guides (shown by broken lines on Fig. 3) and glue a second piece of frilly lace across the ends of the guides, attaching them to these only (Fig. 3(5)). (This will show as pantalets at back (Fig. 4(3)). Spread glue down the length of the guides (Fig. 3(2)) on to the strengtheners (3) and across the top of the lace frill (5). Then very carefully place the prepared back of the toy on to these, right side upwards, taking great care that it exactly matches the front and pressing well in place. If you work with the crossbar on the long stick hanging over the edge of the table, the rest of the toy can be pressed with a flat heavy book until the glue is dry.

Finishing off Trim hair to the required length. Tie a piece of narrow white tape or ribbon round waist so that it covers joins, sticking it in place at front and tying in a bow with long strings at the back. Take the prepared handle, smear glue over the top 4 cm (1½ in), push between back and front of toy at the bottom right hand corner of skirt and press in place until set (see Figs. 2(1) and Fig. 4(1)). With thread that exactly matches dress take a few stitches across top of shoulders from front to back of body at point E on pattern. This is to stop the head sinking down into body.

To manipulate, hold the handle in the left hand and the long stick in the right. As you push the stick up and down, Alice's neck will extend and retract like a telescope.

ALICE WITH A TELESCOPIC NECK

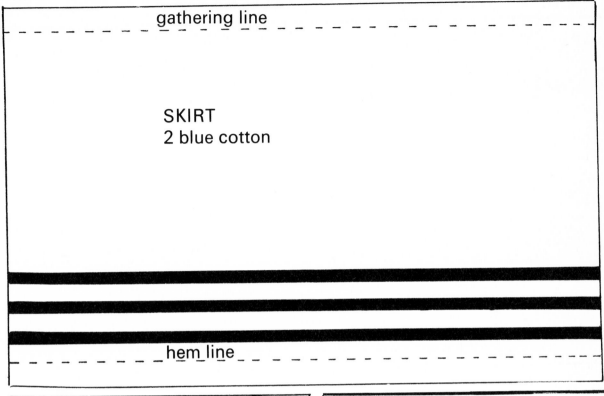

gathering line

SKIRT
2 blue cotton

hem line

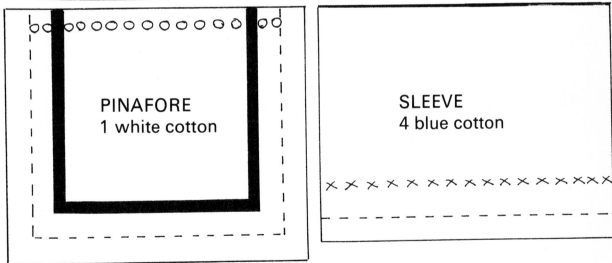

PINAFORE
1 white cotton

SLEEVE
4 blue cotton

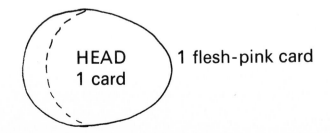

HEAD
1 card

1 flesh-pink card

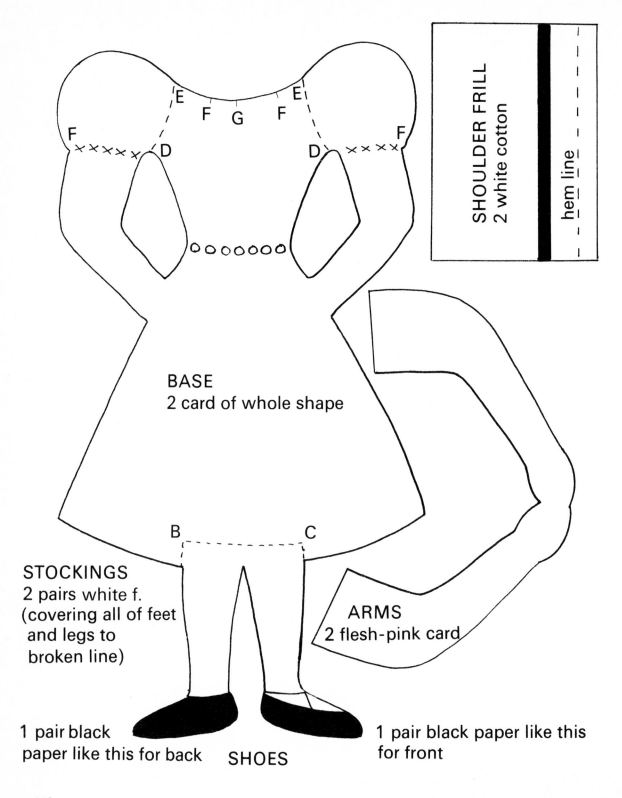

SHOULDER FRILL
2 white cotton

hem line

E   E
F   G   F
F   F
D   D

BASE
2 card of whole shape

B   C

STOCKINGS
2 pairs white f.
(covering all of feet
and legs to
broken line)

ARMS
2 flesh-pink card

1 pair black
paper like this for back

SHOES

1 pair black paper like this
for front

110

THE MARCH HARE

A glove puppet to be held on the hand
Height: 40 cm (16 in)

'The March Hare took the watch and looked at it gloomily: then he dipped it into his
cup of tea, and looked at it again. . . .'

MATERIALS

Light brown fur fabric for head:
25 cm × 25 cm (10 in × 10 in)
Green felt for coat:
20 cm × 41 cm (8 in × 16 in)
Small piece of white felt for shirt
Small piece of yellow felt for waistcoat
Small piece of flesh-pink felt for hands
Small piece of light brown felt for ear
linings and nose
White and brown embroidery thread for
features
Piece of white cotton to line hands and
head

Piece of striped or spotted cotton material
for bow tie
Nylon thread for whiskers
Kapok for stuffing
Adhesive

Optional Piece of corn to wind round ears

METHOD

Cut out the pieces as given on pages 116–17
(32 pieces).

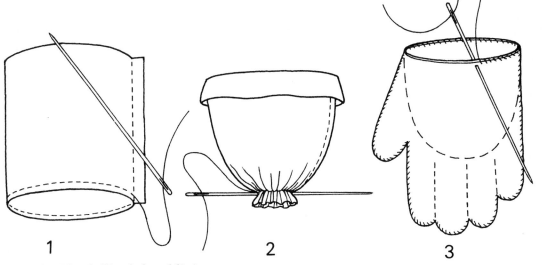

Fig. 1 The March Hare's hand linings

*Coat Sew two tiny circles of yellow felt on one waistcoat front as indicated in pattern to appear as buttons. Place this over other waistcoat front and stitch. Next, position completed waistcoat on shirt front to overlap A-B-A, stick in place with adhesive, then top stitch. Cut coat front only from F-E. Turn back edges of this slit on both sides to form lapels. Lay the shirt front with waistcoat attached underneath the front of coat, stick with adhesive and then sew in place. Put front and back of coat right sides together, stitch seams A-I and J-K on both sides and turn right way out.

Hands Top stitch the two pairs of hands together, making lines of stitching to indicate finger markings as shown on pattern. Cut out hand linings and insert as demonstrated in Fig. 1. Now sew finished hands to ends of sleeves matching letters I and J.*

Head On the wrong side sew gusset to both sides of head A-B, just tacking but not stitching the short section marked 'ear'. Turn and stuff the head, leaving room in middle to insert lining. Sew around the edges of the lining on the wrong side, turn and push this in to the space allowed in the head. Fix the head on to the neck of coat, stitching firmly around both outside of head and lining.

Sew ear linings to ears in pairs, right sides together, and turn. Fold at bottom and insert in seams on top of head at place held together by tacking (see instruction on making White Rabbit page 16). Stitch to

head at positions marked on pattern. Make up the eyes in brown, black and white felt as indicated on pattern, embroider two white stitches on black pupils to add expression, and sew on to sides of head. Top stitch the four teeth pieces together in pairs to make two white teeth and stitch to head following the position indicated. Now make the nose, stitching V-shaped darts together at side and stitch in place on the head. Stuff it as you sew, pushing small pieces of kapok in with an orange stick. With several strands of brown embroidery thread take a vertical line of stitching down from centre of nose to join between teeth, and in the same way embroider a horizontal line along the top edge of the teeth. These two lines will form the Hare's 'lip'. Attach three pairs of whiskers pushing needle through both sides of lip, using nylon thread (see Fig. 2).

Finishing off Sew the two parts of the bow together, then gather in the middle and fold a small strip of the same material around the gathering to give the impression of a knot. Stitch the collar around the base of neck over join between neck of coat and head and fix the bow to centre front.

Optional If you wish to copy Tenniel's illustration exactly, wind a piece of corn around both ears and stitch in place.

Fig. 2 Attaching whiskers

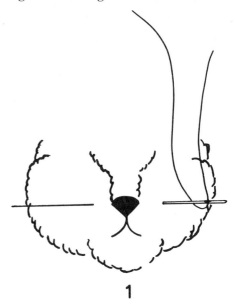

1

1 *Thread whisker double into a long needle. Insert needle into head at place where whiskers are required*
2 *Pull whisker through leaving required length protruding on first side*

2

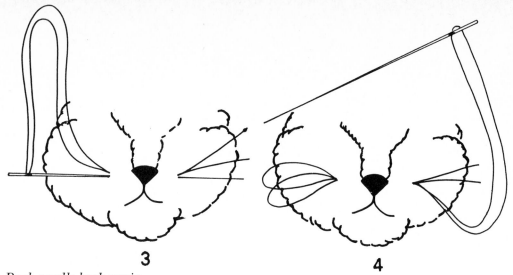

3 *Push needle back again*
4 *Pull needle through leaving loops of the required length on the second side*

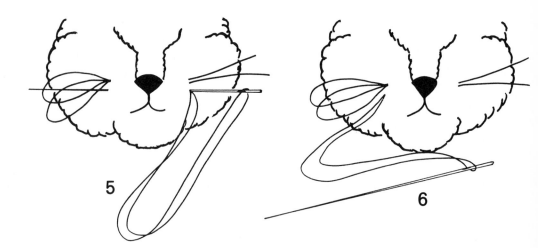

5 *Push needle back again*
6 *Leaving no loops*

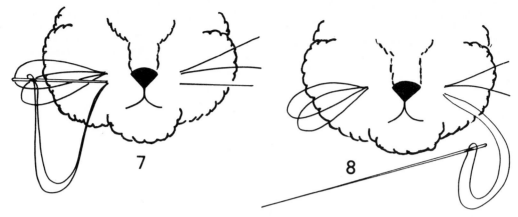

7 Work backwards and forward several
times, leaving no loops, until the whiskers
already made are absolutely secure and will
pull out
8 Emerge finally on the side on which you
started

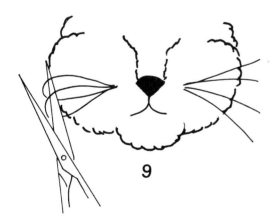

9 Cut off to correct length and cut through
loops. You now have four whiskers each side.
Repeat this process until you have the
required number, using doubled or single
thread

THE MARCH HARE

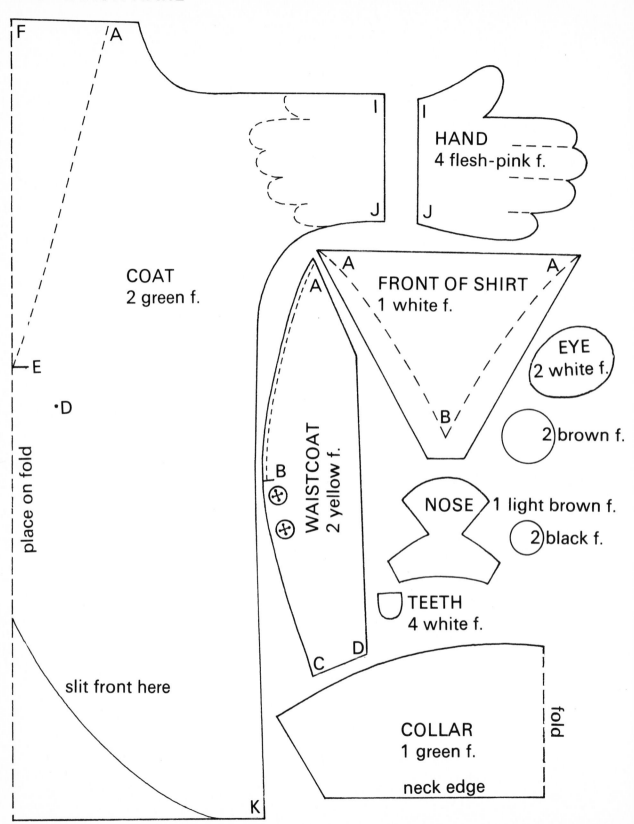

F
A

I

HAND
4 flesh-pink f.

I

J

J

COAT
2 green f.

A

A

FRONT OF SHIRT
1 white f.

A

EYE
2 white f.

E

·D

B

2 brown f.

place on fold

WAISTCOAT
2 yellow f.

B

NOSE

1 light brown f.

2 black f.

TEETH
4 white f.

C

D

slit front here

COLLAR
1 green f.

fold

neck edge

K

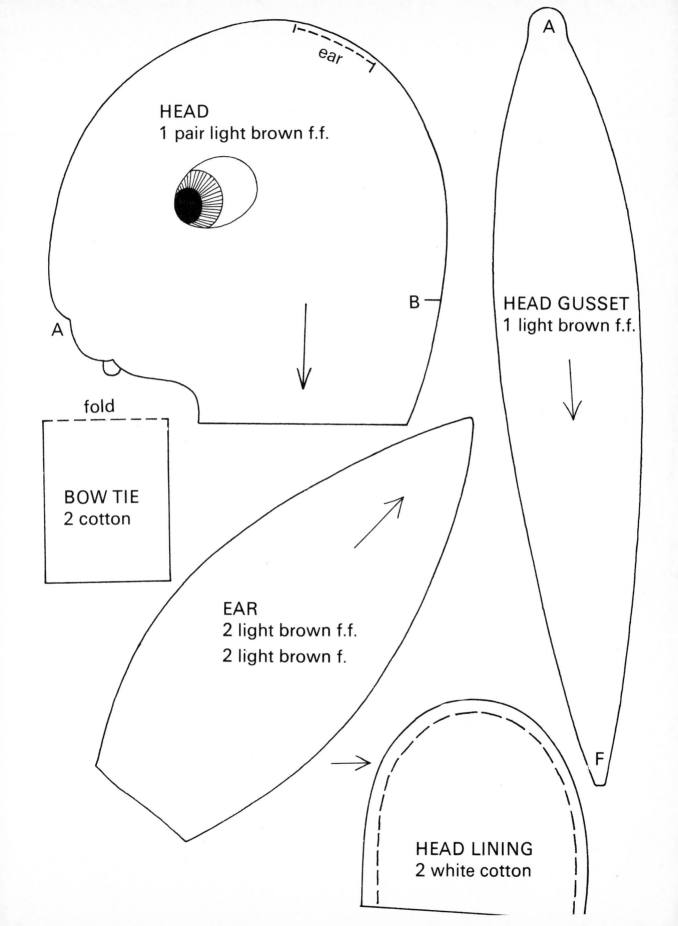

HEAD
1 pair light brown f.f.

ear

A

B

HEAD GUSSET
1 light brown f.f.

A

F

fold

BOW TIE
2 cotton

EAR
2 light brown f.f.
2 light brown f.

HEAD LINING
2 white cotton

THE MAD HATTER

A rag doll (with optional alternative as
glove puppet)
Height: 37 cm (14½ in) with hat

'... said the Hatter with a sigh: "It's always tea-time, and we've no time to wash the
things between whiles."'

MATERIALS

Flesh-pink felt for head and hands:
approximately 25 cm × 25 cm (10 in × 10 in)
Flesh-pink cotton or stockinet for body:
36 cm × 46 cm (14 in × 18 in)
Small-checked fabric for shirt and trousers
(wool/cotton mixture as used for Squire's
coat for the White Rabbit would be suitable:
23 cm × 90 cm (9 in × 36 in)
Red felt for coat:
36 cm × 61 cm (14 in × 24 in)
Fawn felt for hat:
41 cm × 46 cm (16 in × 18 in)
Fawn petersham (grosgrain) ribbon for hat:
about 1·5 cm (¾ in) wide, 53 cm (21 in) long
Iron-on interfacing for stiffening hat
Paper for price-tag:
3·5 cm × 5 cm (1½ in × 2 in)
Small piece of white felt for collar
Small piece of red felt for mouth
Tiny pieces of brown and white felt for eyes
Small piece of spotted cotton material for
bow tie
Small piece of black leather or felt for shoes
Card for stiffening feet
Ten lengths of pipe-cleaner about 5 cm (2 in)
long for stiffening fingers
Four snap-fasteners
Narrow elastic for trousers:
about 12·5 cm (5 in) long

Two tiny buttons
White and red embroidery thread for
features
Brown wool or knitting cotton for hair
Kapok for stuffing
Adhesive

METHOD

Cut out the pieces for the body as given on
pages 122–23 (28 pieces) and clothes (pages
121, 123–27) (25 pieces) making 53 pieces
altogether.
NOTE: Remember to allow 0·5 cm (¼ in)
extra material when cutting out cotton
material for Hatter's body and for shirt and
trousers.

Body On the wrong side stitch the body
pieces together working all round from
A-B, leaving opening at the neck. Then
turn right way out, stuff firmly, turn in
neck edge C-D and oversew. Again on the
wrong side, stitch all round both pairs of
arm pieces leaving straight edge C-D open.
Turn and stuff as far as first broken line V
on pattern, then make another line of
stitching just above this at W (this will
enable the arm to bend at the elbow). Finish
stuffing, turn in the edges C-D and stitch
along broken line at the top to allow the
arm to move freely from the shoulder.

Hands Make up the hands, pushing the lengths of pipe-cleaner into each finger as for Tweedledum and Tweedledee (page 38) but do not twist the ends of the pipe-cleaners together. Pad the hands with a small amount of stuffing and push on to the narrow end of arms at O. Sew firmly to the sleeve, placing a protective piece of binding around where the pipe-cleaners overlap on the edge of the arm.

Legs and Feet Join the front foot pieces on to the front legs E-F on wrong side, then the back foot pieces on to back legs G-H. Now attach soles of feet matching letters I and J and stitch up side seams of both legs. Turn, insert pieces of card cut to shape of soles in base of each foot and stuff each leg and foot, making lines of stitching at X and Y to allow knee to bend. Turn in top and oversew, then stitch along broken line at top of leg. Sew finished legs to body, feet pointing forwards. Sew back seams of shoe uppers and attach to soles of shoes as for Alice (see page 97). Ease on to feet and thread black button thread through holes made with needle either side of centre opening.

Head Place the face pieces right sides together and with very tiny firm stitches sew from neck up around the front to A. Insert head gusset, stitching on both sides from A-B. Turn and stuff very firmly pushing out the cheeks and nose. Fold in neck edge and sew firmly to top of body stitching several times all round with doubled thread.

119

From the back of the head push a long needle through to the front and take a row of tight stitches on the inside of mouth where indicated on pattern. Now sew a row of stitches in red embroidery thread along the straight fold of the separate mouth lining. Stick this line in place inside mouth with adhesive, matching the rows of stitches. Take two small strips of red felt about 0·5 cm (¼ in) wide and stick around both edges of mouth for lips. Take a strip of white felt approximately 1 cm (½ in) wide and fold it in half along its length (it will now be 0·5 cm (¼ in) wide), place over the join between mouth and lips and sew vertical stitches along it with white thread to represent teeth. Take stitches through the head at eye positions, pulling them tightly to sink eyes. Sew the brown pupils on to the whites of the eyes. Place these into the recesses. Stick in position with adhesive and stab stitch around the edges. Attach the eyelids over the top edges of the eyes and embroider brown eyebrows as shown on pattern.

For the Hatter's untidy hair, cut lengths of brown wool approximately 6 cm (2½ in) long, place these together in groups of four or five strands. Double these in half to make loops and sew them to the head, following instructions for Alice (page 95), but stitching them not in line but at intervals all over the head to cover it. Now cut the ends to uneven lengths.

Shirt Working on the wrong side stitch shoulder seams A-B and then sew in the sleeves matching sleeve fronts to fronts of shirt. Sew up the underarm and side seams of shirt. Turn in shirt fronts to broken lines on pattern and hem these, the sleeves and all round lower edge of shirt. Bind the neck edge with a bias strip of matching fabric (see instructions for Alice's petticoat page 96). Top stitch the two white felt collar pieces together at outer edge Z-Y-Z, place the completed collar to neck edge of shirt and sew. Attach two snap-fasteners to

fronts of shirt and stitch in place.

Trousers On the wrong side join the two front pieces at centre seam A-B. In the same way seam back pieces. Now stitch inside leg seams between front and back of trousers, matching points B. Sew up outside seams of legs and make hems at top and bottom of trousers, turning at broken lines on pattern. Thread elastic through top of trousers to fit the doll's waist.

Coat Working on the wrong side, stitch two back pieces together at centre, leaving a slit open at bottom about 5 cm (2 in) long. Top stitch on right side along this seam. Now stitch darts on wrong side of both fronts and back of coat. Join together at shoulder A-B, then sew up underarm and side seams of the coat and turn. Following position shown on pattern, top stitch the upper edge P-Q of the two pocket flaps either side of front of the coat. Attach an extra piece of felt on inside edges of coat fronts to take the strain of snap-fasteners. Cut two circles of red felt large enough to cover the two buttons, gather to close round back of these, then sew over top of one half of each of the two snap-fasteners. Now attach both fasteners to coat fronts.

Hat Cut interfacing to match crown, top and one of the brim pieces of the hat. Iron in position, oversew edges, then on wrong side sew up short edges of crown and attach this to the top, using very neat stitches. Place the two brim pieces together so that the interfacing stuck to one is now hidden and sew these together around the outside edge. Gather inner edge of brim very slightly to fit crown and on the inside stitch firmly in place matching letters A and B. Complete the hat by placing a band of petersham ribbon around the base of brim, making a flat bow where the ends join.

Finishing off Make up the bow tie as for the March Hare (page 113) and attach to the centre front of shirt. Dress the Mad Hatter in his clothes and tuck the paper price-tag inscribed with the words, 'In this style 10/6' into the band of his hat.

Optional You may wish to make up the Mad Hatter as a puppet instead, to make a pair with the March Hare. In this case, make up the coat as for the March Hare from * to *, cutting the same pattern pieces except those for the head, but using red felt rather than green for the coat, white felt for collar, brown felt instead of yellow for the waistcoat and red spotted material for the tie. Now make up the Mad Hatter's head and top hat as instructed for the rag doll, but when stuffing head leave a hole in the centre, inserting lining and stitching firmly to the completed coat as for the March Hare.

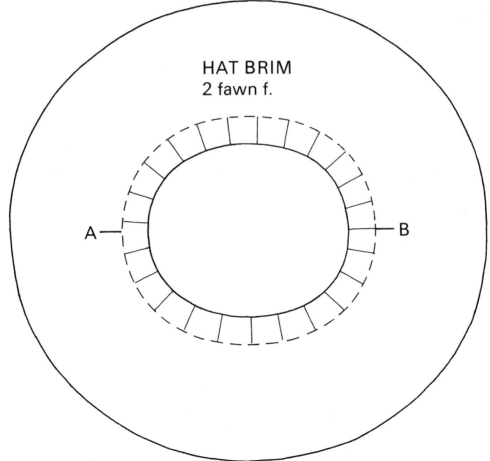

HAT BRIM
2 fawn f.

A

B

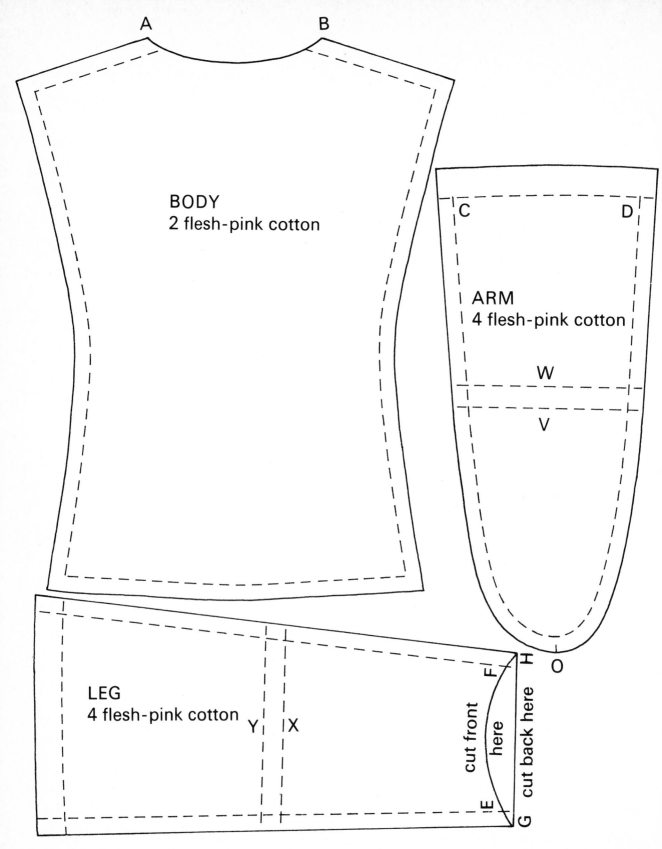

A   B

BODY
2 flesh-pink cotton

ARM
4 flesh-pink cotton

C   D

W

V

LEG
4 flesh-pink cotton   Y   X

F   H

O

cut front here

cut back here

E

E   G

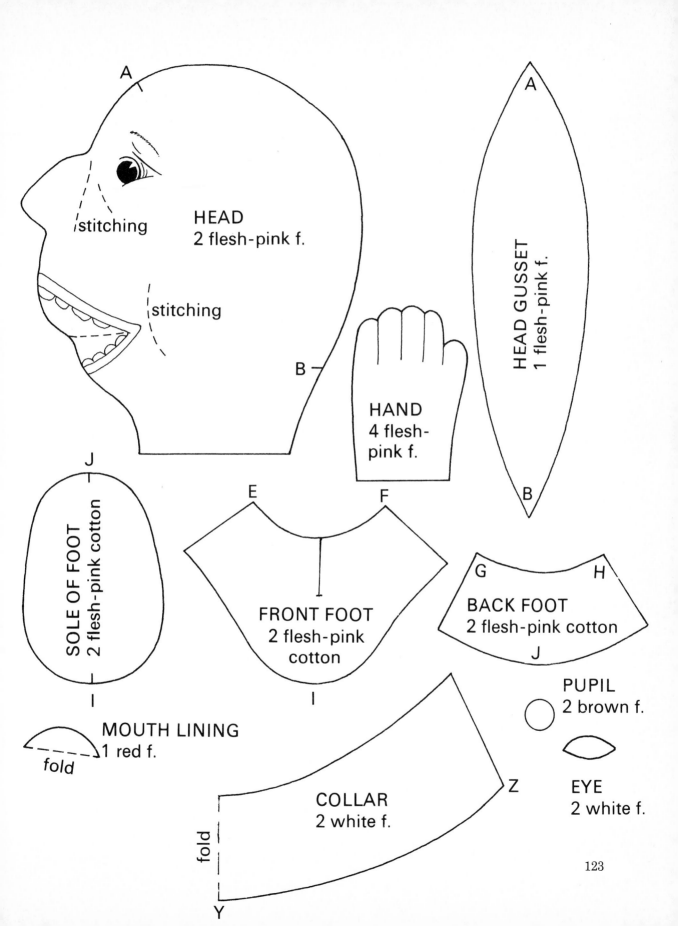

A

HEAD
2 flesh-pink f.

stitching

stitching

B

HEAD GUSSET
1 flesh-pink f.

A

B

HAND
4 flesh-
pink f.

SOLE OF FOOT
2 flesh-pink cotton

J

I

FRONT FOOT
2 flesh-pink
cotton

E

F

I

BACK FOOT
2 flesh-pink cotton

G

H

J

PUPIL
2 brown f.

MOUTH LINING
1 red f.

fold

COLLAR
2 white f.

fold

Z

Y

EYE
2 white f.

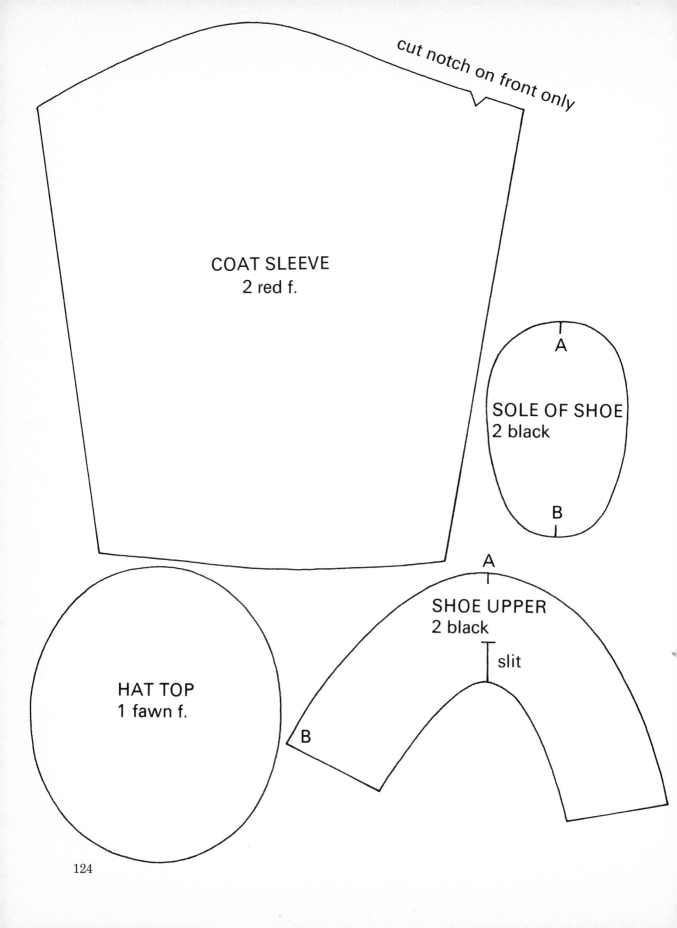

cut notch on front only

COAT SLEEVE
2 red f.

SOLE OF SHOE
2 black

A

B

A

SHOE UPPER
2 black

slit

HAT TOP
1 fawn f.

B

124

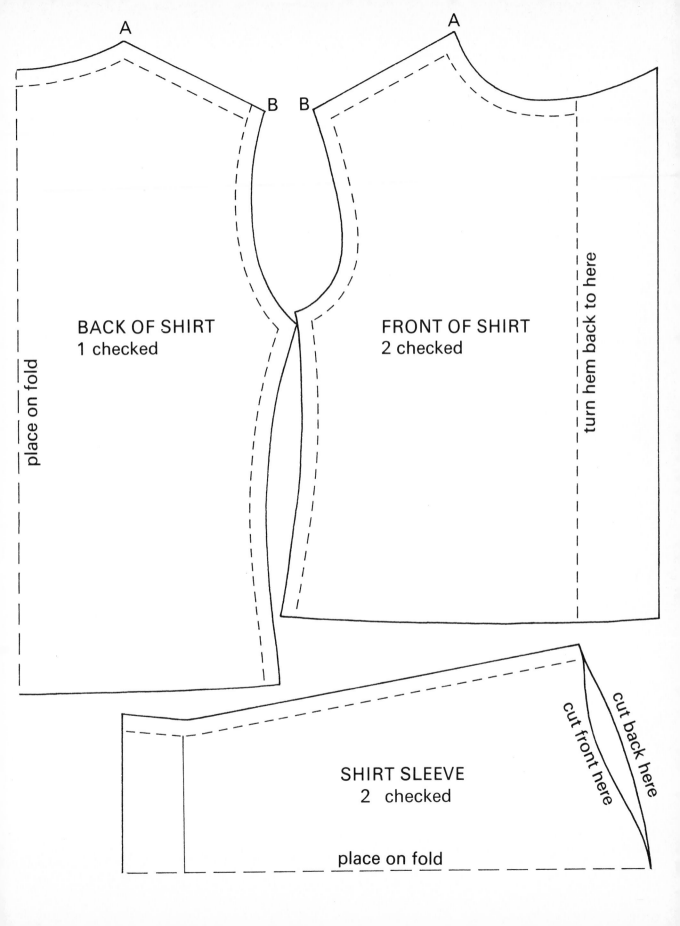

A

A

B   B

BACK OF SHIRT
1 checked

FRONT OF SHIRT
2 checked

place on fold

turn hem back to here

SHIRT SLEEVE
2   checked

cut front here

cut back here

place on fold

THE MAD HATTER

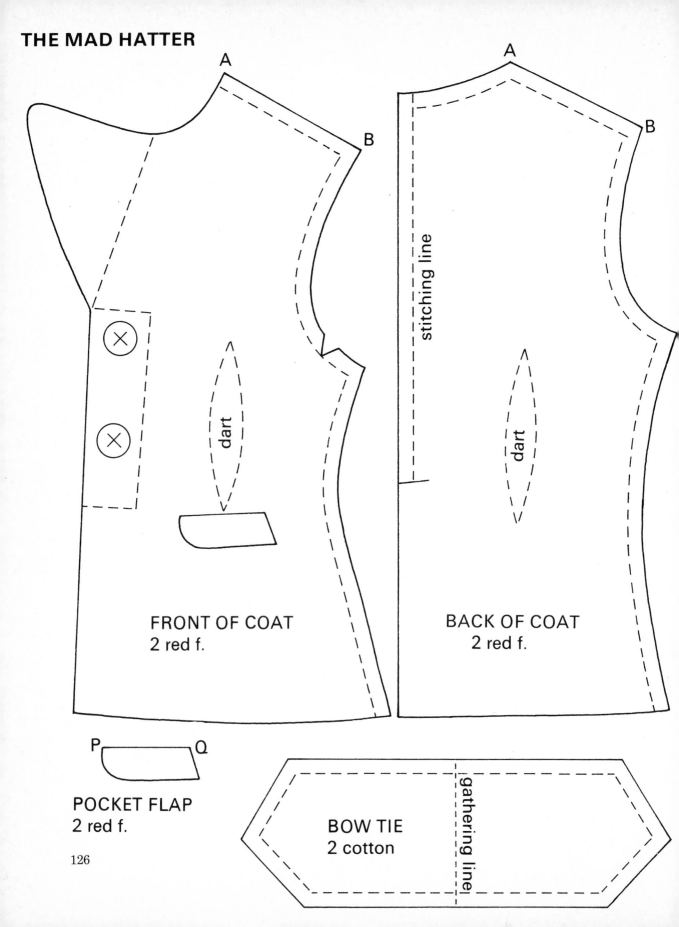

A

B

FRONT OF COAT
2 red f.

dart

A

B

stitching line

dart

BACK OF COAT
2 red f.

P   Q

POCKET FLAP
2 red f.

126

BOW TIE
2 cotton

gathering line